MOSES and the CONSPIRACY of POODLES

Richard Hirschhorn

A Conspiracy of Poodles

Richard Hirschhorn
7491 N. Catalina Ridge Drive
Tucson, Arizona 85718

ISBN: 979-8218-540-401

Can be purchased at:
AMAZON.COM
Bookstore

OTHER TITLES BY
RICHARD HIRSCHHORN:

MOSES AND THE CONSPIRACY OF POODLES

A LESSER EVIL (COMING SOON)

A PRIDE OF HEALERS

TARGET MAYFLOWER

VON EYSSEN DECEPTION (EUROPEAN EDITION)

UNDER NAME OF JON COURT:

LOVE HANDLES

DER GRIEF (THE GRIFFIN)

AUSTRALIA 3 - VATICAN 0

DO ANGELS BLEED

TABLE OF CONTENTS

Moses
and
the
conspiracy
of
poodles

Chapter One

'French Bark'

" Morty, get up. You're going to be late for work." Morty rolled over and checked the alarm clock. It was not lit. The plug was out of the socket, probably when he was vacuuming the night before.The covers were being pulled off his bed. It wasn't until he was on his way home after work he realized his black toy poodle had talked to him that morning. When he got home what was he expected to say to him? This had never happened to him before. He wanted to do the right thing. He didn't want to embarrass poor Moses.

Morty was the custodian or really janitor for the James Buchanan High School about five blocks from his home. It was built in the 1930's of cutting edge school architecture . The architect, recruited by the Roosevelt artists' welfare program, was lacking any insight, creativity, imagination, energy or talent for the project . Dull yellow surfaced brick, rusted metal window grilles, and a geometric boredom, the over crowded school was the light and love of Morton

Haberman. The two matched each with an unspoken passion.

"Hi, Morty," the greeting came from all sides. The children adored him. Unlike other staff, the students never feared him. Caught smoking, or fighting, or teasing girls, or doing anything that would get them a period in Detention, Morty just chuckled and warned them not to get caught.

"Morty," one of the secretary's in the vice-principal's office stopped him. " I just want to thank you for the kitten you gave my youngest daughter. She loves it."

Morty bowed his head and moved on. He hated being praised .He could never think anything to reply. That was the trouble with giving people gifts. They never left you alone after that. He just liked doing things that felt right to do, All the ' thanks' and ' you're welcomes' were annoying. He never asked for them. He never wanted them. They made him angry. He pursed his lips and picked up the pace. He could see the door to his office. Just a few steps, large ones, he would be able to work without being annoyed.

Morty never felt he was an outsider. He regretted the limits of his education. He never allowed that to demean his status. The school was lucky to have him, and he it.

During nice weather Morty ate outside on the back steps with the children. He could be counted on to swap his sandwich for an unwanted raw carrot or egg. Bad weather, he ate inside his little office watching black and white television on an old set with broken speakers.

Once home, Morty checked the mail box at the end of his driveway. He swapped his work shoes for a pair of slippers in the hallway. Mosie rushed to him, jumping and nuzzling and hugging which made Morty feel good inside and all over. He let Mosie run to his outside toilet area between the large oak trees in the corner of the yard. After making certain that no other God's creature had violated his private space, Mosie performed with his usual verve and vigor.

Morty took a can of dogfood from the shelf in the pantry, opened it , scratched a line down the center and placed one half in Mosie's dish in the shrinking square of sunlight on the floor. He was looking forward to his own supper. It was going to be exciting and strange. A 6th grader had lost the chain off his bicycle. Morty had managed to fix the part during his lunch time.The next day, the boy's mother was waiting for him in the Administration Office. She handed him a large flat ceramic dish. The mother said the meal was Spanish. Morty had never spoken Spanish. It was difficult to twist his tongue the name.

The dish had lots of shells and claws and strange parts that Morty shoved to one corner of his plate. He did like the rice; the sauce reminded him of pizza. Mosie came over, but received only a dollop of rice.

"I m not taking any chances with you, young man. We've finally gotten you on a good routine and we're sticking to it. "

" Thank you, Morty, " Mosie jumped up on the adjacent chair, straightened his back and assumed a dictatorial posture. " We have important things to discuss."

" You are talking. I can hear you. Just like this morning."

" Yes, old man," in a mocking voice. " I'm talking. How else could you be hearing me?"

"Dogs don't talk. Something's not right." He shook his head. " Dogs bark. They don't talk"

" Listen to what you are saying." Moses put out a paw to calm Morty. " Let me make this so simple that even a human being can understand. Suppose you visit France and hear all the people speaking French. To you it would seem they are barking to each other. To the French, Americans speaking English would sound like barking . Once you understand French, they would no longer be barking. They would be chatting in English. Same thing happens here. You hear my barking as English. Understand?"

" Moses, I don't understand French. It never sounds like English. It doesn't sound like bark, either. It sounds like French." He was still puzzled. " How would a barking French dog help me here in Ohio? I think you're putting me on. "

Moses shook his head, reached up and gave Morty a nice slobbery kiss which his owner immediately rubbed off. " I love you, anyway," he cooed." Let's move on."

Morty's life, up to now, had been free of mystery and enchantment. Fostered from an early age , he never had a permanent place of his own. The foster parents were decent people, never abused him and treated him with as much love as they could share. He suspected most of them had , like him, come from broken homes. They appreciated whatever warmth a family could give.

When the children would line up to be chosen by new parents, Morty was the last to go. He grew up , missing the earliest years of life with a mother and father. He was almost twelve when his last family adopted him.

Not knowing his biological parents, it was hard to say whom he resembled. He was large limbed, at least six feet, gangly and ill-coordinated when he moved. He had a head of curly dark red hair which trickled down his neck. His ears stuck out like welcoming foghorns. His eyes were deepest blue, his complexion fair with a a network of freckles which would have been more becoming if half had disappeared at puberty. Instead, they begot and begot, until they no longer enhanced, but detracted.

Morty was someone of whom you could honest say had no guile. He was naive, honest and trusting, attributes which never diminished with age.

" Mosie, before we begin," Morty could not believe he was talking to a dog, his dog, as a human being. If the French could understand their dogs barking English, maybe it wasn't all that crazy. The French were always inventing new things, like bread which went stale overnight . He wondered whether barking dogs over there ate it like Moses . "Mosie, let me ask you. How long has this been going on? I suspect you have understood me right from the beginning."

" From the day you found me," Moses shivered."I really don't want to talk about those days."

Morton had passed by a deserted house. The family had moved out. They left their pet tied to a stake in the yard. It had not been fed or watered for days. It had tied itself up in the chain trying to escape. Its hair was matted and insects had infected its eyes and mouth. Morty rescued it, treated it and gave it it water, soap, food and love.They were inseparable from day one."

" Why haven't you spoken to me before?"

"Really haven't had anything important to say."

"Why now?"

" We've been follow........?"

"What do you mean, 'we've'?"

" We, my associates and I"

" What do you mean, your 'associates'?"

" Morty, we have so much to catch you up on. You are a good man, Morton Haberman. You are kind to people as well as to animals. You never ask for anything in return so we decided we should do something nice for you, I'm not the only poodle you have saved."

"Is it too much to ask who these other friends of your's are?"

" Next time we go to the playground, I will introduce you."

" Will I understand them?"

" Just like me. Of course the young ones only talk baby bark. Even I don't know what they are saying half the time."

Morty picked Mosie off the chair and put him on his blanket. " It's probably some thing I ate," he muttered to himself. ' Maybe some foreign spice in that strange dish. This is a dog. It barks. I am a human being. I speak."

Suddenly the doorbell rang. It was his neighbor next door.

" I was watering the lawn. They say to do it after the sun goes down to save money. I could have sworn I heard you talking to someone. I didn't see a car in the driveway so I thought I better come over and check if everything's alright. We haven't seen each other for quite a while."

" I was talking to my dog, Mosie."

"Mosie, " the neighbor rubbed his head and scratched his tummy. Laughing , " What did the little fellow say?"

" He said we have important things to discuss." Morty looked sternly at his dog.

The neighbor looked at the dog and then at Morty and again at the dog. He shook his head, not knowing what to say.

Mosie started barking and moved aggressively towards the visitor.

"He's telling you he would like you to leave."

" Okay. I don't know which one of you is crazier. Morty, take some time to get involved with the community. I can get you into some poker games, maybe a guest at the shooting range. We even have a rugby game if you like to butt heads and break bones. Only kidding, but give me a heads-up."

One bark more and he was gone.

" Isn't there anything you would like to have?" Moses asked. "Something you can't afford but would get if money was no object?

Sure," He chuckled, " My ears. I'd like a full

overhaul. That.... that and changing the screened porch. I would love to change it into a winterized space. What I could do with another room for my orphans."

" Tomorrow is Saturday. Let me get back to the Committee and see what we can do. Trust me. Now, what do you say to some *Haagen-Daaz* before a last pee?

*. *. *. *.

Saturday was the beginning of the weekend off for Morty. He got up, peed, brushed his teeth, gave a light once-over with the electric razor, showered, dressed, opened the fridge, gave Moses the other half of the can of dogfood from the night before, ate his *Rice Krispies* which he liked except for *Pop* who was too loud for that time of day, opened a can of iced coffee and heated it up, smeared peanut butter on two slices of whole wheat bread, replaced Mosie's poop and pee pad for a clean one, picked Mosie up, kissed him while administering the routine matinal belly rub.

It was also an important day for Mosie. He had accumulated a long list of topics for the Agenda. He mastered an extra long pee and poop before leaving. The Doggie Park was not lenient on transgressions.

" Wait here, " He indicated a bench under a large maple tree . " I'll be over there with the other poodles, See if you can pick up a nice human lady ."

It was only a minute or two before Mosie found himself in the center of a group of dogs who had been waiting impatiently for his arrival. They got right down to business.

Large and small, some two to three times Moses' height at the shoulder, Morty's little pet dominated the pack. Morty could see Moses twist his head to point his nose at Morty. One by one, each dog turned to make out the janitor. Morty could swear one of them, a haughty Standard poodle from Judge Steinhardt lifted his head up, sniffed in his direction and abruptly turned back. What was the dog going to report to his companions? Morty felt hurt.

" That wasn't nice," Moisie admonished his friend.

"They have feelings, too.They may not show it, but they know what you are thinking. They have the same five senses that you have, so be nice. Don 't be cruel."

" What kind of a master is Mr. Haberman?" someone from the rear asked. "He seems like a nice guy."

"That's the problem. He 's too nice. He let's everybody walk all over him. He lets the school pay him minimum wage. He works overtime for nothing. His rescued 'orphans' have more room in his house than he has. Personally, I have no issue with him. He is house broken. He cleans up after himself. I get washed blankets once a week. Food is good, but boring . What can I say about a grown-pup who lives on peanut butter? What I'd give for an empty *Fluff* jar?"

" Let's put *Fluff* on next week's Agenda," the same voice came from the back of the pack.

`Mosie took control of the discussion.

" Morty wants to winterize the back porch of his house for more stray pets. He doesn't have the money. He is applying to the Western Reserve Bank for a mortgage. We are going to see 'Chips' Gannon next week. I don't know much about this guy. What if he turns Morty down?

" How can we help him? Any thoughts? " Mosie ran a democratic meeting, according to ' Robert's Rules of Order 'which a Miniature poodle had found in his deceased owner's wastebasket.

" Mr. Moses, " a Teacup poodle piped up." I have a suggestion," she continued apologetically. "

"We're here to listen to anything." Mosie assured. "What were you going to suggest?"

" Gloria, my mistress .... has lots of visitors.. at night."

The pack quickly coalesced around the smidgen dog. Like any group which had worked hard all week, the dogs savored a juicy bone of gossip. The Teacup belonged to Gloria Callahan, private secretary to the High School Administrator . She could not type, nor even read at the level of a graduating senior, but, against a frosted glass panel, back-lit during her hiring interview, she garnered instantaneous approval.

" That is an absolutely odious suggestion, " a golden doodle chimed in after hearing all the salacious tidbits. As a 'partial poodle', the species was awarded a special non-voting status.

In keeping with the democratic nature of the

meeting, Mosie did not permit any discussion. He liked the plan. " Of course we all approve. Somebody move the question. All those in favor?" Paws were held high for approval. Those dogs who had mastered the art of standing on two feet, had the satisfaction of casting two votes. There was no reason to count those ' against '. The motion was carried unanimously.

Chapter Two

' A Tangle of Limbs'

" Do you have any shoes to wear?"

"I'm wearing them."

" No, Morty. Those are sneakers."

" Yes. They're shoes."

" Let me show you what shoes are." Mosie pried open the closet door and dragged out an old dust covered leather shoe. " You can reach for the other. This is going to be an arduous journey."

" What is 'arduous'?"

" 'Difficult'."

" Where did you learn big words like that. Do they come from French bark.?"

" No. From the Webster's dictionary which you use to press your pants. Have you you ever opened the book?"

" It works like a charm to put the crease in your pants. "

" That is brilliant. Martha Stewart keep notice. This man is after your job."

" Who is Martha Stewart?"

" Forget it. I see you got out your white shirt. Nice. Ironed. Now, for the suit. I see one hanging in the back of the closet. Good dark blue. Bankers like dark. It hides their conscience."

" I save that suit for the school Graduation. "

" Put it on. This is an important visit."

" Do bankers really care about how you look to loan you money?"

" This one does. Don't forget a clean handkerchief. Your nose drips without your knowing."

" Can't help it. I have hay fever."

" Well from nine this morning until noon, you will be without any physical blemish other than an old circumcision."

" You've been peeking. No more showers with me. No more."

" Morty, things like circumcisions are not forbidden topics between adult men."

" You are not an ' adult man' . You are just a dog who knows French. As a matter of fact, you are not even circumcised. You should see the way your pee dribbles over your willie when you are finished. It's nasty. Do dogs ever get circumcised?"

"I don't think so. We should drop the topic. It's late. Our appointment is at nine."

" 'Our'? 'Our' ? What's this 'our'?"

" We go together . Do you think that I am leaving the fate of our home in your uneducated hands? Oh, no, honey chil'e . We go together. "

Morty could see the determined look on Mosie's face. " Alright. Just keep still and let me do the talking." It wasn't until they were in the car that Morty realized how stupid that sounded. Mosie just gave a smug grin.

* *. *. *. *

Mosie was out of the car and into the Bank before Morty had even set the emergency brake. The guard loved little dogs. One of his apricot toys was part of the Saturday conclave. He handed out *Milkbone* dog treats like Santa Claus at Christmas . The biscuits were appreciated by canine crowd although Mosie wished the company had gone out of business years ago and *General Foods* invited in.

" Mr. Haberman, you look especially spiffy today."

"Thank you." Morty felt Mosie tugging on the leash. He looked at the large clock on the wall. " Nice to see you, too. " There was no time for conversation. " Wonderful to have your granddaughter this year . Beautiful girl . Which way to Charles Gannon?"

Charles 'Chips' Gannon was of banking royalty. HIs great grandfather had founded the Western Reserve Bank and Trust after the Civil War. His grandfather took over and by the time the Great War to End all Wars was over, it dominated the area. Father Gannon was not so talented . The Depression was one excuse, but fast women and loose money was another. Bankruptcy followed. The Wills family picked it up for pennies when the Second World War was over. Hewing to a disciplined banking etiquette, the bank rose like Jesus on the third day. Father Wills left the bank to his only child, Caroline Matilda Wills. The voting stock was placed in a perpetual trust whose Vestal sanctity was legally guaranteed 'from the dawn of creation to the end of time'

Their marriage was inevitable as Caroline was plain with a club foot and Charlie was renowned for a genetic inheritance reported in astounding inches, no longer in riches. To round out the chromosomal miracle. he was tall, golden blonde hair clipped close like a marine recruit, pale blue-green eyes, and a face which should have been on a thousand dollar bill. They had four children; three daughters looked like Charlie; the boy like Caroline.

Charles was always cheerful. The life of any party, he was a charmer. He had no difficulty in finding penetrable bedmates. His wife knew of his infidelity. She did not care. Charley worked for her. He was skillful in bed . He had honed an amazing recharge rate.

" Morty, " he rose from his chair to shake hands across the vice-president's desk, " or, do you want to be called Mr. Haberman in this palace of commerce?"

" No, Mr. Gannon, Morty is fine."

" This is your delightful little companion?," he reached down to rub Mosie's head with a hard rough swipe. " What is her name?"

" She's a 'he'," Morty corrected.

" Ah, yes, " Charlie inspected. " So sad. Terrible

waste not to have balls to do the 'dirty'. Don't you agree, Haberman? I mean, Mister Haberman."

Morty could hear the low ominous growl coming from under the desk. Moses was in position to take a fierce retaliatory chunk out of Gannon's silk stocking-clad leg.

" Whatever you like, Mr. Gannon. Have you had a chance to look at the Application? I have an extra copy. Gloria, down in the Administrator's Office, let me make copies. She's a very nice lady. Not like the one before her."

Gannon nodded absentmindedly. He riffled the pages Morty gave him. He did not usually handle requests for low budget mortgages. He passed Morty in the halls too often not to take him on. As Head of the School Board he also passed Gloria. At this particular moment in time, he was ' taking <u>her</u> on', at least twice a week.

Charlie scanned, beamed and placed he Application in a tray in the corner of his desk. " Very solid-looking house. Big piece of land. Don't know much about homes in that part of town. Must have been there a long time. Did you buy it?"

" Inherited it. Believe it or not, it was one of those

houses that Sears Roebuck sold in their catalog before World War One. They were originally designed to be shipped by railroad to settlers out west. Grandfather bought one. I still have the order, tucked in the family bible.   All of seventy five dollars. Still standing in good condition. Father put in plumbing and electricity. Needed a new roof at least twice. Added a garage. Has had at least a half dozen coats of paint."

" Sounds like quite a mansion. Why are you looking for a mortgage? I see it's been mortgage-free for some time. "

Morty felt Moses' paw gently stroke his foot. It was the signal to start the sympathy gig.

" It's my other job. I don't mean like working at the school. I don't get paid for it or anything like that. I find animals, pets mostly, who have been abandoned by their owners. I take them in and try to get them healthy again if they need it, give them a good home. I manage to place many of them with families. Most of them are good animals who have run into a bad patch like humans. They deserve a second chance. "
He blushed, " That's what I call my collection, *Second Chance.* "

" What a wonderful service you are giving. More

people should be out doing nice things like that. " He looked at the clock on his desk. " How can I… the bank… help you out?"

" I have a large screened outdoor porch. If I can put in a new foundation and winterize it, I can accommodate more of my 'orphans.' "

A century old house is not what the Bank usually risked money on, especially when inhabited by a collection of emaciated disease-ridden strays. It was a warehouse for wannabe 'road kill.' The Appraisal Committee had already rubber stamped the Application with the ominous large letters, **D. I. ,** which translated to ' Dump it'…, and fast!

Morty waited, so hopeful, it was hard to face him. Charlie tried another ploy.

" How many additional ' orphans' can you accommodate if you can remodel? "

" About twenty or thirty." His hopes rose. Why would Gannon ask the question if he was going to deny the mortgage?"

" Did the town Planning Board approve the plans? After all, it is a residential neighborhood."

Mosie gave a triumphal bark.

" No, it is not residential. Mr. Gannon."

" There must be a dozen housing developments bordering it. " Charlie protested.

" You are too young. Probably weren't even born yet. During the Second World War, President Roosevelt tried to get people to grow food. They were called *Victory Gardens.* Father opened the back acres and let people have plots. The Town Assembly rezoned the whole property as 'farming', They never got around to change it. No problem having animals on the land."

Bite the bullet. Bite the bullet. Charlie's evil angel was prodding him. Move along. The threesome waiting at the Clubhouse is still missing a fourth . Let him down... gently.

" Charlie. The bank is not willing to issue a mortgage at this time. Our Loan Department is stretched thin. Money is tight. Worse situation I have ever seen. A real subprime crisis. We are seeing lots of foreclosures where collateral is sinking in value. Maybe when things ease. More money, we can do business. Not just now. I know you are disappointed, but I want to be your friend, stay your friend, not have to get back to you with bad news if things get worse." He got up and held out his hand.

Morty started to say something. Moses barked and twisted the leash around the chair legs. Morty bent down to free the tangle. He heard Mosie whisper, " Don't say anything. Thank the bastard. Smile. His nose is so long he needs a wheelbarrow to carry it. We leave. Now!"

Morty had no problem with leaving. He couldn't see the connection between a growing nose and a mortgage.

*. *. *. *. *

The next couple of days were grim ones for Morton Haberman. Moses hadn't realized how much affect Morty had invested in the idea of expanding his sanctuary. Moses knew his Committee's plan would succeed. All the details had been worked out except how to keep them from Morty who was the critical component. The timing had to be perfect.

" Don't you have anything to do? You don"t even watch television any more, " Mosie asked. He jumped onto the living room sofa where Morty was resting curled up. The poodle laid his head down on his lap. Morty reached down and stroked his tummy. Mosie purred as much as a dog can purr. " That feels good. I think when this is all over, we need to find a human lady belly scratcher for you."

Morty was still worrying. " You don't understand. Last winter I saw so many shivering animals. This year, I would like to bring them inside ."

Mosie sat up and looked Morty straight in the eye

"Do you trust me? On my word as a pure bred member of *Canis familiaris* species everything will work out fine. I'm just waiting for the right moment . Patience. Patience, my friend."

Morty gave out a deep sigh and hugged his pet. Seeing Morty relax, Moses took a chance. He jumped off the sofa, scuppered over to pick up the television remote in his mouth and brought it over to his owner. Haberman was in desperate need of a good juicy mystery movie to take his mind off defeat.

That Saturday, all the loose ends came together. The only thing the pack warned is to get Morty to the right place at the right time without his knowing why.

"Friday night will work', Moses agreed. " That is my job. You just make sure that you all do your part."

" Why not just tell him, and forget all this Mickey-Mouse nonsense? " a Pekinese questioned.

Mosie stared at the newcomer. " He's too good a man to do the right thing to a bad guy." As the dogs headed out to play on the park lawn, he reminded them, " Five thirty sharp Set it up. "

*. *. *. *.

By Friday, if Moses was more edgy than usual, Morty never noticed. " Hey buddy, " he asked Morty, checking the clock at five fifteen " I have a big favor to ask you. I'm sorry I didn't mention it earlier, but could you take a run down to the school and pick up my blanket we left in your office? It's going to be cold tonight. Be a good fellow."

Morty gave a decidedly unfriendly sigh, picked up

his keys and left. He did not remember leaving anything behind. His memory was accurate. Hard as he looked, there was no stray blanket. He was going to have it out with his pet when he returned home. He was about to start the car motor when he noticed a faint light coming from the Administration Building. He turned off the motor. That shouldn't be. There had been vandalism recently. New rules prohibited occupants after the watchman locked up,

The outer door was unlocked. The light was coming from the Administrator's office. The inner door was unlocked, which was more than could be said for the two naked bodies twisted together.Intertwining was too gentle a word to describe the coupling. Morty did not think of that word or any other to accurately describe the four waving arms and legs. Heaving and grinding, the lovers were oblivious to the intruder.

The flashlight caught the pair at the moment of exquisite disconnect from the real world around them. Ecstatic screams to the Heavenly Father confirmed their state of celestial bliss.

" Mr. Gannon! Miss Gloria!"

*. *. *. *

When the letter came from the Western Reserve Bank and Trust Company approving the requested mortgage, and at interest rates not heard of since the Coolidge Administration, Morty was overjoyed. Mosie was rather blasé about the whole thing after Haberman described the encounter. He apologized about the blanket. It had apparently gotten stuck under the desk. Morty put the whole thing out of his mind except for the strident calls to Jesus and his father at the James Buchanan High School. It was satisfying to know that God was still remembered in the school halls after hours.

Chapter Three

'How to Tell if You are in Love.'

" I 'm in love, Moses, " Morty exclaimed as he came in for supper. " I'm in love, or at least I think I am. Is there any way I can tell for sure?"

Moses looked up from reading the Comic Strip in the local newspaper. He gave his partner a quizzical look, trying to decide on what level to approach the topic. Biological? Emotional.? Historical? He meant have the ' big lecture' with him some day, but no day seemed right to bring it up. 'The day' was here, now, and had to be handled.

" A wise man once was asked that question. He replied, ' if you get an erection.'"

"What is an 'erection'?"

"It's when your willy gets hard, sometimes without your asking it to."

" Then I must be in love."

Moses got up and walked over to Morty.

" How often has this happened?"

" Almost every afternoon."

" Every afternoon? "

" It's been so wonderful." Morty sung the words.

They alarmed his pet." Where and with whom? Not with any of the students, I hope."

" No, no. In my office. With Lavinia."

There was a grateful sigh of relief. What was the assistant librarian of the Zebediah Harcross Memorial Library doing afternoons at the President James Buchanan High School with Morton Haberman, the post-pubescent custodian? Information was needed even if the process required a twelve volt car battery and an inner spring mattress with coils of naked steel.

" Can I explain? " Morty sensed Moses' distress. " Man to man? In terms that even a A.K.C. certified pure-breed toy poodle would understand.?"

" Be my guest."

" As you know, my fields of expertise.."

' Fields of expertise....' Where the hell did this human being pick up a new language? It seems that more than his willy was being inspired.

"......does not include mastery of 'construction', 'building' to you. Lavinia has been been signing out manuals on remodeling commercial buildings ... especially the new dual function split air-conditioning and heating systems . She brings them over and we study them together. " he announced proudly.

"That's very nice of her, but how does your willy get involved in dual function split air-conditioning and heating vents ? I would imagine it is no place for a willy, especially when the current is turned on, although....." A definitely delicious thought raised its head only to be quickly swatted down.

" Lavinia is really very smart . I don't know why everybody calls her a 'dumpling' "

" Oh, come on now Morty. Just look at her."

Moses had a point. Lavinia was about five two, when in high heels. A large round moon face, clear complexion with a small pug-nose. A pageboy haircut of bleached blonde hair. She wore a tight blue silk jacket and skirt, all very business-like. The skirt was short and failed to hide thighs whose walking friction could have lit fires in an arctic blizzard. All her shortcomings were more than compensated by the décolletage which advertised lush hidden pleasures from milky breasts and rosy nipples.

" I think she is adorable."

" Adorable?."

" Yes. She thinks the same of me."

"Has she ever actually said so? Called you

'adorable'?"

" Not in so many words. I do think she likes me more than any other girl I've met."

" Then, I am happy for you."

Morty picked up the little dog and gave it a big noisy kiss on its tummy.

" Mosie, she's in trouble. The Police came by to interview her." His eyes were full of tears except for a few which rolled out.

Moses was suddenly at full attention. Drama rarely rattled this orderly home. Was 'dumpling' in trouble? Every fraternity brothers' wet dream? The delicious rewards of saving her? Riding to her rescue on a white stallion, escutcheons and pennants waving in the breeze? Just fantasizing could unleash a flood of testosterone. What was the problem? One doesn't risk life or honor for something trivial.

Morty was not helpful.

" All she did was was cry and huddle in my arms. She never told me what the problem was. Maybe she is too embarrassed. Mosie, you're good at these things. Help me. I really do love her."

" Okay. Okay, already. Let me think." He got down on all fours, then lifted his butt high in the air, head touching the floor.

" What are you doing?"

" I'm thinking."

" In that crazy position?"

" Yes, in that crazy position. Do you have any idea how your body thinks?"

" Yeah. You give the problem to your brain and it thinks and gives you the answer."

" The brain takes at least twenty percent of your energy. Twenty percent of your blood and oxygen . This position guarantees the blood will go to your head. Try it sometime, maybe when you are doing crosswords."

" Does it work?

" You're damn right, it does. Now, I need you to do something."

" Okay. What?"

" I want you to break a window in your office."

" Why would I want to smash a window ?"

" There, I knew it. If you had been down here with me, with your rear end in the air, you wouldn't be asking such stupid questions."

" I always knew you were trying to be a 'smart ass'; now you have proved it. Get up here Moses and give me a 'heads up', forgive the pun."

" You're getting better. ' Heads up'. 'Ass'. Pretty advanced there, buddy, If you want to get information involving a crime that could send one to prison, where would be the best place to get information?"

"Television?"

" Not bad. Where else?"

"Newspaper?"

" Very good. Anything more?"

" A police station."

" Bingo! You are an 'interested party'. You need an excuse to get inside and talk with them. They won't disclose the investigation to some bum sitting on the curb"

" Oh… I see…. Officer….my window…. It's been broken… I 've been vandalized. Okay. No problem. What are you going to be doing while I commit perjury?"

" Friedrich is the Police Station dog. He and I are going to have a nice quiet conversation. He's a rather well-groomed aggressive German Shepherd with ancestral roots in Stuttgart."

Morty worried. " Don't take any chances. I don't want you to get hurt."

" You mean with Freddy? Don't worry about Freddy although he has, though, a rather unbecoming prejudice against little dogs. "

" Why?"

"He thinks they are smarter and superior to him."

"Is he right?"

" I know we poodles are. I never let it show, unlike some of the others, so we get along."

" Do you have an interpreter?"

" Why would we need an interpreter?

" You're a French poodle and he is a German Shepherd. Do you understand him?"

"Of course, why wouldn't I?"

" Different countries. Different languages."

" Morty. The dialects may be a little off-putting. We dogs are all the same species. If we can have sex with each other, why shouldn't we be able to speak with each other ?"

" We humans are all the same species and can have sex with one another, yet we can't speak with every one."

" That's because in your case, civilization hasn't caught up with your evolution. The centers in your brain to love your fellow man are less advanced than those to oppose your thumb."

*. *. *. *. *

Morty had never been to a Police Station before. The high chain-linked fences, glaring yellow paint lines with arrows pointing everywhere except to a vacant parking space and loud speakers shouting instructions to prison buses coming and going, were both exciting and forbidding .

" Go, play, " he told Moses, who scampered to the grassy patch along side the building. " I'll look for you when I get out."

" Okay, boss. Be brave. Cowards die a thousand deaths; heroes live a thousand years. "

" Let's narrow that down to thirty minutes. I don't need the Bible thrown at me."

" God, " Mosie whispered to himself, " you can

always tell a no college education. It shows."

The   German Shepherd rose to his feet. He thrust out his right paw in a rigid solute ' Heil.... I mean 'hello.' "

Mosie held out his hand for a shake. "I'm Mos....." He was about to call out his Judeo-Christian name when he realized   'Mosie' might be more appropriate and safer.

" Are you a reporter?"

" No. I'm....."

" A liberal do-gooder? You know the kind I mean. Always trashing moral values and the gold dollar? "

" No. . None off those. I just need some information."

"Doesn't your kind, always."

A little put out by this hostile reception, " What do you mean, ' my kind'?"

" You know," he brought his head closer. Mosie pulled back a foot or two for safety. He wished to return home with both of his ears."A 'pink-o' Commie bastard always sniffing around, hoping to find something to sell to the media without paying for it."

" How about some *Cheese Whiz* and *Ritz Crackers*?"

" You're the man. "

Morty had left the tailgate down for ventilation. Once aboard, Moses realized he still didn't have the Shepherd's name.

" It used to be 'Adolph. The guys wanted something less Germanic. It's been changed to 'Fritz' or ' Fritzie'. I don't like it, but I had no vote. So much for democracy." He gave out a big cheesy burp. "So, what can I do for you?"

Mosie looked up again at the dog. He knew exactly how to interest him. " Why would the *Gestapo* be after her."

*. *. *. *.

Morty was eager to hear what Moses had learned. His own expedition had been worthless. He never realized that because he was a careful honest American citizen who obeyed all the laws, paid his taxes on time, accurate to whatever *H. and R. Block* determined, never reviled his neighbors, kept his radio and grass low and celebrated with reverence all legal holidays , he was of no use to the constabulary.

Not only was he denied the ear of a big-shot, but he wasn't even allowed to approach closer than three feet in front of the Intake Officer. He was given , unrequested, a personal escort back to his car where Mosie waited. As he drove out of the yard, Morty could still hear the mellifluous tones of 'come again.' He recalled the warning of Will Rogers, Jr., ' just be thankful you don't get all the government you pay for.' Oh, how right!

*. *. *. *.

" The first thing the officers at the Station said was

' what a dumpling'."

" Let's get past that." Morty scowled.

" Okay.. Okay. " At first opportunity, Moses needed to put his butt up in the air. "The men at the Station refer to it as ' The Case of the Missing Maps.' Most of them have read Agatha Christie and imagine they're the reincarnations of Sherlock Holmes.

"One day, Mrs. Hedecky, the Head Librarian ,came to them with a concern. It seems that some valuable books had disappeared from the Archive Collection. They were a gift from Harcross, the fellow who had founded the Library and given money as well as his personal collection which included the missing ones."

" What was so special about the books? How long had they been missing?"

" They contained maps of the Spanish explorations of the southwest, where the missionaries had settled , where soldiers made contact with the native tribes, where waterholes and battles were located. Wonderful histories of the Spaniards trying to document their ownership of the land. The Church sent the books to Mexico City where the monasteries preserved them. After the Spaniards were driven out, the books were stolen and sold on the open market.

They must have changed hands many times until they ended up with old man Harcross who left them right here."

" How valuable are they?"

" To you and me, I mean you, not me. I'd swap them all for a good jar of *Fluff*. In today's market, I learned, over a million dollars each. That's a lot of *Fluff*."

" Okay, the books are gone. Since when?"

" That's part of the problem. The books were there on August tenth ."

" How do you know? What happened on August tenth?"

" A twelfth grade class at the high school was doing a class project on Willa Cather. The teacher brought the students over to look at the maps.

" Ah, yes, ' Death Comes to the Archbishop.' "

" What? '

" Forget it, Just reminiscing on a book from my childhood."

" Were the books there after the tour? No little kiddies took them home for their project ?"

" They were there. Mrs. Hedecky was certain."

" How did they discover that there had been a

robbery?

" About a week ago, the Library got a request from a museum in Atlanta to borrow the books for an exhibit. They were missing."

" So, nobody knows how long the books could be missing. They were there on August 10th and disappeared sometime after that. "

" Who had keys to the Archive?

" At first, it was only Mrs. Hedecky. There weren't funds for an Assistant Librarian. Volunteers helped clean the building and put returned books back on the shelves."

" What about the Archives?"

" She took care of that herself."

" How many keys were there?"

" There were two keys. Mrs. Hedecky had them both. There had never been any duplicate keys made that she was aware of."

" Was there another way into the room?

" None. The space was designed by the architect specifically for the collection .He made sure it would be isolated."

" Any surveillance or security protection?"

" No . Now the place is wired like the Mona Lisa.

I don't think you can take a book off a shelf without a Swat Team squashing you to the ground."

" Then, my girlfriend arrives as Assistant Librarian."

" When is that?

"' About a month ago. I 'll have to get you the exact date."

" Mrs. Hedecky gives her a key."

" No reason not to. Her References are top notch."

" That's it. They could have been taken before Lavinia came, which would clear her, or been there and removed by her or somebody else after she started."

" Were they insured?

" Only as part of the General Contents Policy. Nothing specifically for those three. The library only gets a few bucks a book. "

" Who's been called in to investigate?'

" The local police. "

"Isn't there some national task force like *Interpol* to contact ?"

" The Library didn't want to advertise the disaster. The Annual Drive is coming up and it would be bad publicity."

" Understod. They must have done some investigation."

" They did. The two librarians are what is called, 'persons of interest'. The Police checked references, mail, bank statements, email messages and all other cyber stuff. They searched their homes, cars, all with their approval. Talked to neighbors. Nothing could be found. Both of them are in the clear."

" Thank goodness."

" No, " Moses said softly, afraid to voice the words, " One of them is guilty."

" How do you figure?"

" They both had means and opportunity. Mrs. Hedecky even had the good fortune of Lavinia joining the Library to introduce a second suspect."

" You left out motive."

" That's obvious."

"Obvious? Not to me."

" Money. What else? Unless they are both candidates for advanced degrees in Southwestern studies, what other earthly reason would anyone have to steal the maps?"

Morty got up from his chair. He lowered himself to the floor and posed with his butt up in the air, belly on the ground.

" What are you doing?"

" I'm trying to think. Isn't that what you said helped you?"

" Morty, in your case, considering your anatomic evolution, you would have to stand on your head to achieve the same result. I start with an advantage. You'd have to do a total one hundred and eighty degree flip. Get up. Stop being silly. Let's reason this out like two sensible poodles."

" Okay, Mosie, I am trying to think of other solutions to the problem."

" Don't. Einstein once said that if you do the same experiment over and over, and, expect a different answer each time, you are a fool.

" We have the facts, or at least, enough to work with. There's only one thing we don't know. Where the books are. Find the books and you've found the culprit. There are two possibilities. One is the Library itself. What could be better than concealing the books on the shelves, in other bindings or jackets? I'm sure the volunteers would help search. The risk for the criminal is that a book-by-book search would discover them . "

" And the other"? His butt still up and ignored by Moses. " That, my friend, is the mystery. Remember, the criminal or criminals must hide the books away from his or her personal space . The location must be accessible. It must be convenient to retrieve the stolen items. While waiting to recover them , the location has to be unsuspected."

Morty slid down. His anatomy had accomplished its task. His eyes met Mosies'. They nodded their heads unhappily in agreement. They needed no further experiments. Gravity had done its work.

*. *. *. *.

That afternoon Morty drove over to the Library and asked for Lavinia. She came out, gay, bouncy and eager to see her boyfriend.

" I can drive over here tomorrow after work, and return the books you signed out for me. Mrs. Hedecky will want them back for the book count. I'm busy tonight grooming Moses. Maybe....," he reached for her tiny hand," ...maybe tomorrow we go out for supper?"

Lavinia hesitated for a moment. She saw Morty's eagerness and agreed, placing a wet kiss on his cheek. "*Delphi*?"

" Yes, why not?"

Morty had no great love for spinach or lemon in his food, especially when layered with what seemed to be a white custard. This particular Greek restaurant had cute little waiters in ruffled aprons and pointy shoes. When they saw her enter, they raced to take her table. She definitely was a favorite , especially when she leaned forward to read the menu with her short-sighted eyes.

"Okay. I'l pick you up after work."

" Can't wait." She bounded up the stairs, waving her hand behind her.

The happy couple had much busywork to do this evening. None of it involved passions of the heart.

*. *. *. *. *

Morty could not help reflecting how alive the school was during the day ,with hundreds of students and teachers popping in and out of classrooms. There was a constant background of noise.... voices, bells, loudspeaker announcements, doors opening and closing, youthful voices shouting to be heard above the din. Now, it was silent as the grave except for the ventilation system turning on and off and telephones ringing with no one to answer them . It was dark, no lights, no moon, no stars.

Morty and Mosie hid behind a collection of large grass mowing machines.They crouched down, invisible in he shadows. They hoped things would move along. The hide-out was not particular comfortable for humans whose knees did not fold up conveniently as did canines'.

There was a muffled noise at the door. It was always kept unlocked. Morty felt if anyone wanted old equipment that badly to steal, go ahead. He did have a handwritten sign on the nearby wall which warned:

He who takes
What isn't hisn't,
Must give it back
Or go to pris'in.

A weak beam from an old flashlight led the intruder to a stack of library books on Morty's desk. The intruder made a rapid selection, dropping the unwanted ones on the floor. With the three archive books under her arm, Lavinia was about to leave. She stopped, frozen in the glare of a dozen lights from the Police.

"We will take those books from you now young lady, if you please," one of the officers said, deftly removing them from her embrace.

What happened next was a series of unhappy events which Morty hoped someday he could erase from memory.The room was swarming with blue-clothed bodies intent on seizing the young girl and holding her still. Countering this noble goal was one angry 'dumpling', kicking , writhing , twisting, and biting, all while screaming obscenities that were jarring even to adult ears.

Finally restrained , handcuffed , and placed in the hands of the Police Matron, Lavinia directed her last curses at Morty who was catatonic, eyes wide open, limbs frozen, mouth agape. His thoughts flashed on and off like a broken neon sign.

" You pathetic little nothing. You disgusting dirty loser. How could you even think I was interested in you? You disgust me," she snarled as two detectives literally lifted her off of her feet and dragged her to the patrol car.

Moses took in the action. He had already anticipated the cruel scene. He knew Morty would take the brunt of the hate Lavinia was spewing out.

" Let's go home, my friend," he urged. " There's nothing more we can do here. If they need us, they know where they can find us."

The drive back was like carrying a carload of elephants. They were there in the backseat and had to be dealt with.

" I thought she was really in love with me. She was just using me. I suppose sooner or later she would have left, without saying a word."

"I would guess that was her longtime plan. I wouldn't be surprised if they find she is part of some gang that goes around the country stealing valuable items from local museums and libraries, where security stopped withJohn Wilkes Booth."

" She seemed so sweet and loving. Nobody had ever treated me that way." He turned to Moses and repeated softly, " You know I really loved her. I would have given her the books and helped her escape."

" Even after you heard what she said?"

" Even after what she said."

"I know, Morty. That's why wisemen say that 'love is blind'. I wonder whether the tears that follow are to wash away the blinders?"

*. *. *. *. *

Mrs. Florence Hedecky at work was not Mrs. Florence Hedecky at home. Her apartment was on the top floor of the only condominium residential building in this conservative town of historic battle sculptures and dead generals. The lobby was all white with spotless marble floors, the walls white granite with grey grained streaks. Alcoves glowed incandescent lights over abstract geometric blocks and spheres.The reception desk and elevator doors were sheathed in stainless steel. The elevators cooed as they called out the floors.

The doors quietly slid open opposite the Hedecky door. Moses noted that there was only one apartment on each floor. He wondered why the lady was working forty eight tiring hours each week for a pittance. Balzac warned that behind every great fortune was a crime. What was her's?

" My late husband, Richard ,was a well-known architect. He liked to design municipal buildings, city halls, government offices, bus depots, hospitals. Nothing fancy to tantalize the public eye. He did extremely well and left me more than comfortable. He also taught me to have a trained eye for beauty. I finally settled on a contemporary look. No bric-brac. No gingerbread to fill up voids.Only what is needed to do the job of living and nothing more.:

The apartment certainly bore out her fashion ethic. The furniture was modular, with thin chrome legs. The

ceiling lights were flush or else concealed .
Thick tightly woven grass mats were placed to block blinding reflections from the highly polished marble floors.

In the background, a short trim lady of middle age and asian features busied herself, flitting from kitchen to dining room, finishing up last minute details.

The hostess herself, had on a pair of black silk trousers cinched in at the waist . A blouse of creamy ivory satin, open collar and extra wide sleeves which fell over her wrists completed the outfit, except for a lustrous double string of *Mikimoto Acoya* pearls circling a wrinkled neck.

She welcomed Morty by extending her hand. Flustered, not knowing the correct etiquette, he reached out and shook it. The hostess did not embarrass him . She gave him a quick kiss on both cheeks.

" Morton," she drew back to take in a practiced once over, " Thank you for your help in restoring my treasures. The Library Association also sends their appreciation. We would like to honor your deed by giving you a lifetime pass to the Library, including the Archives. I hope you will occasionally go in and see what you rescued."

" Thank you very much,"Mosie added an appreciative bark at this point.

"You'd think he understood what we were saying ."

"Oh, I'm sure he does in his own way. "

" I got the signal from Mrs.Ling. Dinner is served. Would you please take my arm, Morton? We have prepared a dish in the kitchen for Moses." She knelt down and gave him a affectionate rub around his neck. "I have a little Cavalier King Charles Spaniel bitch, so he won't be lonely"

" That is very nice of you. "

What happened next was not quite as thoughtful.

" I hope you like what we have prepared for you. Richard loved this dish. He said it reminded him of a good home." She lifted up the tureen cover releasing a flood of fragrant steam. "Aha, " she smiled, " dumplings!"

Chapter Four

' Mosie and his E.S.S.'

" Who was the first president born in the United States?"

No answer.

" Who was the first president born in the United States?

" I don't know and I don't really care. Washington? Jefferson?"

" No. Martin van Buren."

No response.

" He was born in the actual United States. The rest were born in the British Colonies."

`" I suppose."

Morty started reciting poetry:

'Many and many a year ago
In a kingdom by the sea.
There lived a girl whom you may know
By the name of......?'

Dead silence.

" 'The name of Annabelle Lee.'"

Nothing .

Morty started singing:

' Jingle bells. Jingle bells.
Jingle all the way.
Oh, wha......'

Moses looked up and gave his roommate a disgusted look. "What with all this stupid nonsense? Singing? Poetry?"

"Well, you need something. You've been moping around this house like a nun in a nudist colony."

" I don't need anything. Please, do your clown routine somewhere else. Why can't you just leave me alone?"

" That's what I've been doing. Doesn't help. You just lie there. Don't eat. Don't read the papers. Don't get upset who has the t.v. remote. I wish you were thinking so you'd put your ass up in the air. It'd at least be a change of scenery ."

" Then, all you would do is complain about my farts."

" ' Passing gas,' Moses, ' passing gas ' . It has a nicer ring to it. "

" A fart is a fart. Old Benjamin Franklin wrote a pamphlet on the subject. ' Fart Proudly.' "

" The problem with your farts is that they are lethal. They sneak up to you in a quiet, stealthy way. One minute you are healthy and the next you need oxygen."

" Your's aren't much better. "

" At least we give warning so you can run for cover."

"Warning? What good is that when you are half paralyzed? Like a paraplegic escaping on a scooter." He slumped again and assumed the fetal position.

Morty knelt down next to his friend. He rubbed Mosies' top knot. " Tell me, old man, what's bothering you? Are you having pain? Can I help?" He picked Moses up and put his arms around him. " You've been losing weight, haven't you?" He paid no attention to Moses' vigorous denial. He carried him to the bathroom where they both got on the scale together. He put Mosie down and got on the scale himself. He calculated the difference. " I'm right. You've lost over a pound and a half. Tell me what's going on or you are going to the vet."

*. *. *. *. *.

Morty never minded sitting in the waiting room, although Moses continued his apprehensive shivering.

" Don't worry , little man. We are not going to operate on you. Just a visit. Relax." He hugged him even closer, almost enveloping him in his arms with just the nose peaking out.

Doctor Daniel Wychinski, the Second was a perfect image of his father, short, early balding, square face with prominent jaw, and dense black eyebrows matching the halo of hair on top. He had thin lips permanently creased in a smile and a closely shaved beard. He was a joker, always skirting the nice with impudent hints of the naughty, which endeared him to the blue rinse ladies who flocked to his office with cats in various states of obscene obesity.

His father had died of kidney disease barely a week after his son's graduation from veterinary college, a coincidence which had evoked years of commiserative offerings from his patients, most of which resided in Pyrex dishes.

" At least he died happy, Doctor Daniel."

" That he did, Mrs. O'Halloran. That he did, I'm sure, like Mr. O'Halloran." One would have sworn the doctor hailed from the 'ole sod'.

" I did try my best to make him happy. I did."

" Just like you are trying to keep Liam here happy"

" I do, Doctor, I do."

" I know you do."

" Double portions may keep him happy, but they shorten his life. You want to keep him around for a long time, don't you?"

" I do, Doctor, I do," squeezing the monstrous Angora in her arms.

" Just remember, if he passes, you will be all alone. Think about that. I'll give him a check over shortly."

Morty loved it. Dr. Wychinsky was the only vet who came out to greet all his patients before seeing them. Of course, this allowed him to double his office practice. The frivolous patients got a quick scheduling; the serious ones were expedited to the larger Diagnostic Suite.

"Oh, Doctor Dan, " the still unmarried Brearley sisters whispered as they offered up Babe and Bob, the twin canaries who were pooping too much. " How do you stay so young.?" The Brearley sisters had been 'young' themselves since Doctor Dan inherited them from his father years ago.They had a secret crush on Doctor Dan.

" Just promiscuous sex. Just steady promiscuous sex." He gave them a wink. " You two maidens look as if you are been getting some deep protein infusions lately. Is that true? "

" Oh, Doctor Dan, you shouldn't talk to us like that.We're just good Christian ladies."

" Did I ever tell you the joke about the the good Christian lady with the two female parrots who kept yelling out,' we want sex'. we want sex '? She brought them to her priest and explained the problem. The priest said that he could fix the problem. He had two male parrots who spent all day clutching their prayer books and praying. The lady agreed to place her parrots in their cage. As soon as they entered, yelling ' we want sex', the male parrots dropped their books and shouted,' our prayers are answered.'"

" Oh, Doctor Dan…", but the vet had already moved on.

" What brings this slugger here?" He asked Morty.

" He's not himself."

" He looks pretty good to me."

" His spirits are down, if you can say that about a dog."

" Why can't you say that? You know, dogs are really an extension of ourselves." Moses barked in absolute agreement with the statement. " How have your spirits been, Morty?"

" I've been fine, Doctor. " Morton protested, a little put out by the vet''s attitude.

" Okay, let's see him. " He bent down and picked Moses up. " You know, little man, thanks to your owner's unhappiness you are going to be poked and probed and drained of blood. Blame it all on him."

Moses loved it when Doctor Wychinskhy talked to him like Morty did, except expecting no answer.

" Alright, Slugger, what do we have here?"

Moses squirmed in the vet's arms. He did not like

to be called 'slugger'. It was not only embarrassing, but demeaning. He imagined everyone in the office looking at him with pity, seeing his empty scrotum and the lifetime of joys denied . How would Doctor Danial Wychinski the Second like it if he was castrated and people called out him, ' hey there, baby maker', how they hanging'?

That would have been a fate worse than death for Daniel Wychinsky the Second, heir apparent to the city throne of Catholic Father of the Year. Beaten out of first place two years running by a local ophthalmologist, he had resorted to resting two bags of frozen peas on his testicles at night.

Moses was poked and probed and drained of blood for a screen of a dozen medical parameters of health . His weight was down over a pound and a half. His poop analyzed.His pee collected . A total body cat scan was scheduled. The total bill exceeded Morty's weekly salary, even before deductions for withholding taxes , social security, Medicare, unemployment, workman's compensation, and state taxes .

" I have a feeling everything will turn out fine," Doctor Daniel the Second comforted. This was a mixed blessing as Morty was still trying to put aside a weekly sum towards plastic surgery for his ears, an anatomic anomaly excluded in the Municipal School Group Insurance Plan.

" What do you think he has? Some tropical disease like Ebola or Monkeypox." Morty had been advised of those dangers on the nightly newscast.

" No. Nothing like that. " He picked Moses up and left the room. " I'll be right back."

CANCER. That was all Morty could think of. Why discuss his diagnosis without inviting the patient to learn of its demise.?

" I know it sounds silly," the vet explained when he returned sans Moses, but I think dogs feel some of our emotions when we discuss things of this nature."

" It ...is...cancer.."

" Nonsense. Nothing of the sort. You know, Morty, symptoms of loss of appetite, confusion, depression, withdrawal, apathy, are not limited to dogs. Women have them, too."

" Yes, it is called ' men o'paws.'"

" Not quite. It is called ' menopause.'"

" Yes, that's what I said, ' men o'paws."

" It's only for women."

" Why do they call it a man's disease?"

" Well, it's a long story. Let's get to that later. Anyway, it's for women. You get it when the sex hormones begin the change."

" You think Moses is changing his female sex hormones?"

" He doesn't have female sex hormones, only male ones."

" Okay, you think that Moses has picked up this female disease?"

" No, not exactly. I think he is experiencing the equivalent which dogs do get, especially small energy breeds like poodles. It's called ' E.S.S. ' "

Morty wasn't sure how to respond. His brain tried every combination of words to fill in the blanks, to no avail. Nothing sounded canine and ominous.

" It's the 'empty sac syndrome.'".

Morty looked perplexed.

" Let me explain. That's why I thought it better if Moses wasn't here. You and I don't have it. At least I don't. I hope we never will. You check. Make sure everything is still down there ."

Morty furtively slipped his hand down to reach his crotch and smiled.

" Okay, Morton, that's enough. You can take your

hand out now, if you please. Save that for later. See how pleased you were with yourself? Can you imagine going through life without such comforting companions?"

Morty gave another sheepish smile. It was probably the first time in his life that Morty realized how good it was to have two warm buddies that never left his home without him.

" We don't know how much of a dog's psyche is tied up with his testicles. Of course, his desire for sex is muted. His desire for fatherhood is thwarted. If a dog had even a few percent of what you and I feel, it must be earth-shattering to lose them."

" Why now?"

" That is an easy question to answer. You know we figure a dog's life by a multiple of our's. Judging by Moses' age, he must be at puberty. You know how nasty boys are at that age. In the shower room, for example, they love to tease and humiliate their friends if they are different. Think of the daily disgrace heaped upon poor Moses when he is out in public. It must have worn him down to the point where he cannot cope with it any more."

" That's so sad. I'm happy it isn't cancer or

multiple sclerosis or schizophrenia or something like that. It must be terrible for him. No wonder the poor fellow couldn't tell me about it."

" What do you mean, ' tell you about it'? Do you two have locker room sessions together.?"

' I mean I could tell by the hurt in his eyes."

Doctor Daniel Wychinski the Second sat down on the edge of the treatment table next to Morty. He closed the file.

" There is something that will help Moses. It has just come along. It's something that men have had available for many years....fake testicles."

Morty was by now way out of his element. He was torn between squeamishness and curiosity.

" What we do is operate on the pet. It doesn't require a full anesthesia. Just something to make him sleepy. We use a local anesthetic to block pain in the area. We make an incision , a really small one, and insert the prosthesis. It doesn't take more than fifteen, twenty minutes.

" The patient can go home as soon as he wakes up. No need to take the stitches out. They dissolve on their own. We'll give you some pain pills. He won't need them for more than a few days. Then, the patient can go out into the world swinging his new balls like the clabbers on the Liberty Bell and just as joyful."

Morty didn't need to hear and wasn't interested in the gory details. He sat next to the Doctor, swinging his feet back and forth, protecting his crotch as inconspicuously as he could.

" If you think it is the right thing to do, I'm for it. I'm not the patient here. Moses is. It's really up to him. I don't see why he would object, but we really shouldn't operate on a patient without his consent."

" Morty, we are talking about Moses, a pet, really a dog."

" He is a patient, and a most important one to me."

" He is going to give consent? He is going to sign the legal permission forms? He is going to pay for it?"

Morty realized that he was in a bit of a predicament. " Of course not, doctor . I am. Mosie is such a real member of my family that I often forget he's just a poodle. He will, however, give consent."

" Well, after you two have your mysterious séance, call the office to book a time. He won't need a pre-op examination. Today's will suffice. I have done dozens of these procedures. The results are great., I promise it will restore Moses' *joix de vivre."*

He got up, shook Morty's hand, signaled for the nurse to come in and discuss the pre-op instructions and the fee which could be paid in four equal installments with interest on the remaining balance tied to an average of the preceding twenty four hours European LIBOR rate. Despite what Doctor Daniel joked about, Morty intended to have a serious talk with his poodle that very night.

The operation was not new to Mosie. He knew of several members of his Assembly who had been operated on. The results were so natural that Mosie never gave them a second look. He was all for it.

As expected, the surgery went well, the postoperative course went well, the skin sutures dissolved on time and Moses' *joix de vivre* sprouted anew. Prancing and jaunting with his back legs spread further apart, his newly swinging *Scrotties* heralded to the world that a newly-minted hero now bestrode its broad boulevards.

Chapter Five

'The War Begins!'

The letter lay between them like a primed land mine, about to go off and shatter their tranquility. Moses shoved it barely a millimeter towards Morty who pushed it back, even less. They knew this letter was coming. Their neighbors had already received their's. They were prepared for it, as much as recipient of a Cassius Clay body punch could know in advance where the next blow would fall. The envelope kept moving like a snail with a faulty sense of direction.

" Okay," Moses finally accepted the envelope and extracted the letter.

May 14, 2024

Warfield Community Developments Ltd.
4246 Happiness Drive
Mundego, Illinois
886421
Att: Mr. Morton Haberman
14 Forest Glen Pathway
Middletown, Ohio

068973

Dear Mr. Haberman,

I hope you have heard about the dazzling future that Warfield Developments has planned for you . I am certain, by now, you have experienced the everlasting thrill of knowing your town will join the expanding list of 785 communities we manage, give or take a few.

Please review the 6-color print literature we are enclosing. Appreciate the incredible marriage of town and country so artfully integrated in our developments. Lot sites are always carefully planned to protect each and every homeowner. An accompanying Home Owners' Covenants and Conditions which run with the title guarantee the sanctity of this harmonious balance. Prices vary depending upon size and location. Warfield has always felt the obligation to facilitate home ownership through its Credit Subsidiary, when required.

We expect to have a demonstration sales office near the center of town. Do not hesitate to purchase a Warfield home of your dreams for your children and their children.
Come visit and feel the joy.

Sincerely yours,

Marshall K. Warfield
President

MW/ca

" Do you 'feel the joy '? ", Moses asked sarcastically, " or is it the other way around, ' feel the dazzle 'and ' see the joy'?"

Morty picked up his car keys. " In either case, I 'd like to see how this vision of Mount Olympus is coming to grace the town. How about our going down to the Town Hall to see this heavenly vision?"

Moses slowly rose. He gave a vigorous stretch, his rear end rising gracefully up in the air and his front legs way out in front of him. He gave two yawns , a very silent fragrant fart and waited by the front door.

* *. *. *

The Municipal Records and Deeds Annex to the City Hall building was a delightful relief to the eye. Unlike the squat yellow brick relics of the Civil War it was designed completely of glass, with three walls which met at the corners to make a perfect triangle. No matter where you looked, you had the wonderful option of seeing through the building to the trees outside which surrounded it, or else watching the people inside move like a living frieze of motion and color.

" Let's try the Planning Department, " Moses suggested.

They handed the letter from *Warfield* to the

Receptionist who directed them to an office in a corner of the building where they could almost reach out and touch the forest. It gave a wonderful sense of peace. Not so, the news they heard. The clerk was a young, pudgy frumpy girl whose subsiding acne and noisy bubble gum marked her as a recent hire. She ran her eyes over the *Warfield* letter.

" Yes? I see these all the time."

" What we would like to see are the Plans for the development."

She collapsed a bubble which was destined for the Olympics until it ran out of air.

" Where's your other letter? The Certified. One?"

" This is the only one we got."

" You need the official notification from *Warfield*."

" Why ?"

"It shows the County Land Listing, the Plat number, the lot dimensions, along with water, sewage, electricity availability. It also shows the Fire District and distance to the nearest Schools and hospital. It reports all recent sales and prices , foreclosures, mortgages and intra-family transfers. "

" Sounds like quite a mouthful," Morty commented, thinking of suicide from multiple sticks of gum blocking an airway.

" The law requires that all abutters receive this information. I need to check off that you got the letter to prove you have been legally notified."

" I'm sorry, miss, but we never got it. This is all we got, " holding up their *Warfield Development* letter.

" Sorry. I can't let you in, Come back with the official letter so I know you have been alerted . It's really for your protection."

" I don't even know where the land is. Is it breaking some Papal Bull for you to tell us?"

" I can show you." She took them into a small room holding a miniature display. The streets were narrow; the houses small; the fake pedestrians strolling on the cardboard sidewalks not necessary, because there, as striking as one could see, were the apartment buildings and shopping malls filling the field belonging to *second chance* .

Morty was carrying Mosie in his arms. The poodle had a good look at the layout. There was an involuntary exclamation , " What the f.....?" Morty was certain the young maiden had heard it. His only hope was that she did not understand. His own understanding was strictly anecdotal.

*. *. *. *.

Jerry Hermann was one of the town's most successful lawyers. If you were absolutely innocent, you went to one of the second tier attorneys and were usually acquitted. If you were absolutely guilty, undeniably guilty beyond a shadow of a doubt, you went to Jerry .The results were the same. Morty had jump-started Jerry's Mica Blue *Land Rover Rogue* on more than one frozen School Board afternoon. Besides, Jerry loved to tell dirty jokes and needed an audience and laughs ,which Morty always provided even when he didn't understand. .

Jerry was in his forties, He was short, stocky, bull neck (from his days as a welter-weight in college), square face with deep beard-darkened crevasses, wide nose with flaring nostrils, and eyes fronted with thick eyeglass lenses. He was definitely unattractive. If the rest of him had least a *soupçon* of adorability, his thick hairy coat would have crushed the attempt. The black' happy trail' started where it supposed to start. It migrated north up to eyebrows, growing in strength with the distance covered. A sort of reverse Newton's Law of Gravitational Attraction. To add to this image, at age 34, Jerry was totally bald, like his father and probably all the Hermanns before him. However, he was a damn good lawyer, like his father and probably all the Hermanns before him.

" I' ve seen the letter you got from *Warfield*." He suddenly noticed Moses. He got down on his knees and took Moses in his arms. He cradled him for several minutes stroking his head, his back, and finally his stomach."Oh, I needed that. Nothing like a tummy-rub after a day of malingerers and cheats and killers. Oy! It's a good thing that Mrs. Hermann doesn't know how I made a living." He stopped the rubbing, and lay down on his back. He placed Moses on his abdomen and said, " Now it is your turn, little man. "

Moses responded to this endearment with a satisfied sigh , closed his eyes and promptly went to sleep.

"What's his name?

" Moses. I call him Mosie for short."

" This is your lucky day, Morty. How in the world can I ask a retainer from the owner of the little furry monster who brought the Israelites out of Egypt into the land of Canaan? " He lifted the poodle to his neck and held him like a baby for burping."

Mosie raised his head, " Morty. We have a winner here."

" You certainly do, Mosie," echoed the lawyer.

" You understand bark?"

"Certainly do. You'd be surprised how much information I get from my pet. He belongs to a Saturday group of pets that act like the Sherlock Holmes' *Baker Street Irregulars,*"

" Is he a bulldog?" Moses asked.

" What else?"

" Black, with a white blotch over his forehead and on one paw?"

" That's Igor."

" I know Igor. "

" I'm sure you do. Igor speaks of you often. Let's get down to business. "

Jerry got out a dish of water for Moses, some *Orange Crush* for Morty and put several pads of paper on his desk.

" If you do nothing, you will lose the land. You will make a lot of money, if that is what you want. In any case, you will lose the forty acres."

" How can they do that?"

" You know that Statue of Justice over the door on the Court House, the one holding the scale. She's blind. That's why you are going to lose. Justice has no way of seeing evil."

Morty was upset. " Why did I come here? I might as well tear down the fence and invite *Warfield* in."

" Ah, Morton, that is where I come in. You don't think I would let you lose a field for this handsome poodle to pee and poop in? The Second Law of Thermodynamics says, if I remember my third grade, that an object in motion, will stay in motion, unless acted upon by an outside force. I think I got that right. *Warfield* is going to bulldoze his way to get that land, by hook or by crook. I am going to deflect him from his cause. You, my friend, will help me stop the *juggernaut*, by hook or by crook. "

Chapter Six

' Morty and Moses Face Defeat'

" I'm smart, Morty, but I'm just one lawyer against a whole phalanx of lawyers *Warfield* employs. He has dozens of developments. Probably hundreds of lawsuits going on at the same time. Most are frivolous, linoleum wearing out, toilets overflowing, but some are serious, you know, foundations cracking, gas furnaces killing babies. Those are expensive to defend. With juries loving the underdog , the trials end in big penalties . *Warfield*, I'm sure, has set up reserves to settle the nasty ones. Insurance will cover the rest.

However, trials get headlines. Headlines are bad for business . Bad for the stock price. *Warfield* acts like a stealth bomber, fast and invisible . It gets in there and rapes without anybody noticing. It gets out before the enemy finds out it's pregnant."

" We could send Moses in on a glider and a bee-bee gun."

Hermann ignored the sarcasm. He loved to tell stories. He had his little speech planned out and insisted on carrying it through without interference.

" We can either attack him head on or...."

" Excuse me if I stop you. What is ' head on?"

" We buy a few shares in his company. We become an irate stockholder, seeking truth and justice. We start lawsuits alleging that Warfield is a syphalylitic philanderer, an abuser of women in his office, a druggie who snorts cocaine and peddles heroin. His developments are incubators of disease, rodents, tuberculosis, AIDS. His roofs leak; his walls are covered with mold; the company is in default of city taxes, that sort of thing,"

" Sounds good to me," Moses piped up.

" No, my little friend, it doesn't work. That's why I get the big bucks and you get kibble.
Sooner or later, *Warfield* agents will discover who is behind it. They'll get the sympathy vote.

" Still , I still think it sounds good," Moses protested.

" Here, Mosie, take some string cheese and just listen."

" Instead of a sledgehammer, we bleed them with mosquitoes until they leave. One pin prick after another until it no longer makes sense to waste money and time here. There are lots of other towns to rape. You don't have a federal monopoly on forty acres of dog shit and grass."

Morty patted Mosie who was still upset at being called out. Not only are poodles allergy-free and adorable, but they have thin skins and egos.

" Right now we need some bones, a few quashed bullets and some corroded coins,"Jerry told the pair.

" Let's get started. "Moses urged. On this , there was total agreement.

*. *. *. *.

If Mrs. Hedecky was surprised to see Morty and Moses visit her at the Library, she didn't show it. It was closing time. The Library was empty. The Librarian was going through the building, turning off lights, checking the locks on the doors. The ADT Panel with the newly-installed security system still puzzled her. She held the Service Manual in one hand as she figured which switch to turn red, which switch to turn green, and which light, when lit, warned her she had exactly thirty seconds after it was activated to flee before being electrocuted.

She recognized Jerry as one of her most dedicated cardholders when he was in school. She had a group of students whose diligence marked them as ' most likely to succeed'. She felt a source of pride when some of them rose to prominence. Jerry was one of the Chosen few.

" What can I do for you, Jerry and Morton?" She petted Moses who ran off looking for the bitch.

Jerry got right to it. " After the Revolutionary War, people moved west. Ohio was part of the Western Reserve. The Indians weren't happy. The government sent troops. I think that one or more battles took place right here."

" So history says." Mrs. Hedecky said, delighted to discover book learning was still relevant." Usually it's just an oral history recorded from years back. I suspect with all the commercial and residential building going on here, no one wants to find anything that will block growth."

" We do."

" Come back tomorrow morning. I have to take

my Spaniel home and feed her. She is overweight, but if I don't give her supper, she thinks she is dying and plays dead on the sofa. Let's find the bitch. You take Moses. Tomorrow. I have coffee. You bring the doughnuts."

"Incidentally, Mrs. Hedecky, during the Civil War who won the Massacre at *Chillicothe*?" Mosie asked.

" Really, Moses, no one wins a 'massacre."

" Somebody must have been the least massacred," he insisted.

" There were more Union soldiers left alive than Confederate ones."

" What a shame."

"Why a 'shame', Mosie?" Morty asked.

" Well," Moses answered, " Some days I think of how nice it would be to have a private slave to do all my bidding."

Morty gave him a slight blow to his head.
" You do, you little ingrate. You have me."

The next morning, the Librarian was as good as her word. Even better, Moses mused. She must have arrived at least an hour before their scheduled time. She had assembled a tray of assorted artifacts for them to examine. Someday, Moses thought, I have got ask her why she works so hard. He had heard her husband left her well off . He doubted she was serving time under a Court-sponsored Community Work program.

" You should find these interesting. " She spread out the items. "Most came from the Massacre at Chillicothe. I wouldn't be surprised if the same soldiers met again here. "

"What's this?" Morty held up a sleek shiny brass cartridge case.

Moses pulled his arm down. " It's twentieth century, Morty. Probably from a hunter looking for rabbits in the field."

Mrs. Hedecky took it back. " Here's one you can use, " holding up the squashed remnant of a lead musket ball.

The hour passed with Jerry putting the battle specimens in an envelope. " We all thank you for your help. Is it okay to come back if we need more items?"

Mrs. Hedecky beamed at the thought of future breakfasts with guests." Of course. Anytime. Now you go hide them and find them for the second time."

Jerry patted the poodle on his head. " That's your job, young man."

*. *. *. *. *.

The problem of a true-to-life discovery upon the verdant field of *Second Chance* was the main topic of conversation at the Assembly the following Saturday. Just dumping the Chillicothe relics on the ground was not even brought to a vote. The land had been combed for over one hundred and fifty years. It was doubtful someone would not have found a bone or piece of shrapnel.

" How about burying them again?"

That, too, was voted down."

" Too obvious," Moses said.

What at first seemed a simple question had unexpectedly defied a logical solution, until Santa, a humongous Newfoundland belonging to Mr. Santos, barber-elect of the neighborhood, spoke up.

" The oak tree in the corner," he turned his massive body like a giant weather vane, pointing to an ancient tree in the corner of the property. It was hanging over the fence onto Santose' garden. It was barely alive with only a few branches sprouting green leaves. At some point in the past it was hit by lightning bolt which split it into two parts. Torn asunder by an act of God, neither half had managed to survive on its own. Most branches were dead or supported by other branches close to dying. The twisted roots were exposed and bleached by sunlight.

" That tree needs to be cut down, " A observant dachshund decided all on her own."

" Yes," Santa continued, " Guess what we will find in its roots, hidden all these years?"

There was a moment of silence. Then came wave after wave of pawplause, Despite his bulk, Santa was swarmed with his mates until it looked as if he would be submerged and drowned by the goodwill.

With Morty's blessing, Mr. Santos was delighted to order an arborist to remove the tree. It was nightfall by the time the deed was done. The following morning's inspection revealed a tangled nest of roots and earth holding enough evidence to delight the heart of the Ohio Historical Society and poison that of Marshall K. Warfield.

*. *. *. *. *.

When *Time Magazine* interviewed the President of the *Warfield* empire, the only fact that they were able to get was that he refused to use the 'III' that he was entitled to. Not even when pushed would he concede that neither genetics nor legacy had any role in his success. It was his drive alone, his genius and his determination that had created the empire. After the Second World War, M.W. the Second had predicted the boom in housing from the returning veterans. Cookie-cutter construction and unimaginative designs were acceptable, as were the cut-rate prices he charged.

When stress, fatty foods and thin women ushered him through the Gates of Paradise, his son left Princeton and took over the reins.

The days of pinching pennies in anticipation of another Great Depression are over, he told his Board of Directors. ' Do you know why?' he asked just before firing them and converting the company into an LLC. They shook their heads.
'That's why you are an unneeded bunch of stupid asses," was his parting answer. ' Because those

customers are all dead or in nursing homes'.

Luxury. Convenience . Amenities . A LIFESTYLE their parents could only have dreamed of before shuffling off into death or decay, or both. We will mow their lawns for them in the summer, shovel their snow in the winter, chlorinate their swimming pools, oil their treadmills, trim their flower gardens, stock their libraries, lull them to sleep with lectures, movies and jazz bands. Throw in curved sidewalks, golf cart lanes, tennis courts, concerts, cooking lessons, and calorie-counting counselors.

It was a new, unique concept. Like *McDonalds,* M. K, sold the homes on reasonable terms, but kept title to the supermarkets, drugstores, service stations, coffee shops and big box stores which, for astronomical rents, were guaranteed no competition for anything they wished to sell.

No dividends were paid on the few shares which had escaped capture. Paperclips were recycled. Executives drove repossessed *Pintos,* as did their boss. M.K. was just as thrifty in his personal life . One wife, married young and kept around. One frugal pre-nup. One child, male or female, whatever . If needed, extra sex got rented by the hour, like his trucks.

Thin, buzz cut silver/grey hair, steel-rimmed eyeglasses, lean chiseled facial bones and lips so thin they appeared surgically removed. He did not tolerate fools gladly.

He paid his executives well, after they had signed strict non-disclosure and non-compete legal documents. Few left to join competing companies. M.K. was an icon... a god. How many mortals in this man's world were privileged to glow in his penumbra?

The telephone call at 4:11 in the morning was not unexpected. It was after M.K. had completed his morning run, taken his shower with a healthy wank, emptied his bowels, finished his steel-cut Irish oatmeal, and started phoning his well paid executives.

Wes Wasserstein knew the call was imminent. He got out of bed, quietly, not to waken his pregnant wife He went to his study, eyes barely open, hand hovering over the telephone to grab when the bulb flickered.

"Yes, boss. Good morning to you, too. Shower good? Run nice? Bowels open? Peggy is good... thanks for not asking. Regular is good. Stay on the oatmeal."

"What about that cow ditch in Ohio?"

" Memo on your desk ."

" If I read the memo, I wouldn't be wasting my time calling. Bottom line... is.. what?"

" Shitheads blocking."

" Kill'm! Glad Peggy is doing okay. Give her my best. If you need anything, leave memo...." The call disconnected.

Wes went back to bed. Peggy rolled over to spoon, hand resting on his genitals. 'What the hell, ' he thought.'Why not?' He doubled his legs together to pull off his pajama bottoms, pushed them aside, gave himself a few vigorous strokes, raised her upper leg and deftly slid in. For at least three minutes in and four minutes out, Marshall Warfield and an Ohio cow ditch had vanished and life was good.

*. *. *. *. *.

7:30..... Wes's car turned into the '$1 - Day Parking ' lot

7:42.....the parking lot attendant dropped him off at the airline gate.

7:45.... Wes turned in his economy ticket at the counter, added three times the price on his American Express Card and swapped for a First Class ticket.

7: 59....Wes pushed his pre-loaded carry-on into the overhead compartment three rows down, returned to his own row, swung down into the seat, fastened his seat belt, ordered two bloody Marys, and resisted the persistent mental image of a cow patty. Any residual glow from a 'leg-over' had long been left at the '$1-a-day' lot.

Giving the cab the address of the *Warfield* office, Wes settled back, feeling the onset of not enough sleep and too much tomato juice.The office was the company's store-front sales display showroom. Wes barged in the back room . He plopped down on a couch whose relatives graced over fifty identical showrooms.

" Where's Lester?"

" Here, boss. " One of over 70 full time and part-time lawyers on the national payroll, Lester Farrell wanted to ' make his bones'. So far, all he made this fiscal year was a measly eighty seven k and one acne-riven virgin.

" We have to get rid of the 'farm ' designation. I

started a suit against the city to restore it to a ' residential' classification we can build on. It comes up for review in two weeks. "

" What's the strategy?"

" The original Federal Land Grant gave the pioneers forty acres to ' settle'. No requirement to 'farm;' they could start a distillery if they wanted. The city voted a ' farming' designation during the 1940's as a reward for Victory Gardens. This allowed a lower tax status. We believe the case is moot as the city ordinances cannot supersede and void a Federal law. That is our case."

" Lester. Why am I here?" The fog was lifting, only to be replaced with anger. He needed to get back to civilization.

"The fuckers went around this and started this battle shit to get the land reclassified under the Federal Historic Sites Act. That Act protects like Mount Vernon and the Statue of Liberty."

" And?"

" I queered that up, too. The Ohio Historical Society was finally able to show that there were no soldiers, Union or Confederate, within a hundred miles of this shithole after the Chillicothe Massacre. "

Wes sat up. " Lester!" He almost roared. " Why am I here?!?"

"It's blind."

"Blind?" His voice was plaintive. "Who?"

" 'Not 'who'. 'What'"

" 'Who'. 'What'. Just tell me. Please." he pleaded. He wondered if the city was ' dry'. If not, could he get a gallon of salvation delivered to the back door?.

" The mole. It's blind. That's why you are here."

Whatever inner sinews of strength and off-the-chart Mensa test scores made Wes Wasserstein a personal pick of Marshall's suddenly came to the fore. He deliberately slowed his breathing . One bottle of ice water from the fridge. Half inside him and half over his hair and face, did the trick.

" Tell me."

" Moles are not blind, despite what people think. They just have poor eyesight. This one is totally blind. It can't see, for shit."

" It lives in the forty acres and is on the short-list as an endangered species."

"How did you know? The National Geographic Society just sent out the News Letter."

" That Lester is why I wear a solid gold diamond

Rolex and you some plastic shit."

Lester did not wear some 'plastic shit', but figured if he still wanted to make eighty seven K and an occasional acned virgin, he'd better keep his mouth shut.

" Okay, Lester, here's what you're going to do,." He whispered in the lawyer's ear. If all went well, M.K.'s best and brightest could take care of this piss problem in no time. " Expense it so the I.R.S. won't find it . Hide it so these hillbillies don't find it. Then, go home. We need you ' as pure as the driven snow,' or "as pure as' Caesar's wife', which ever your college education taught you. Get the guy. Pay him well and disappear. Play golf or tennis or fuck your wife for several days straight. Don't contact me at Central. Forget I was ever here."

All Lester could remember over the following weeks was ' pure as the driven wife'; which made no sense at all.The sex was okay.

Back home, cushioned by his wife's swelling belly, Wes could not recall how much it cost to open the door to the cage and let the poor mole go free. A few bucks to the watchman or starving college student on night duty was cheap. M.K. should be happy; he never did like pets. Wes hoped the animal made it home safely. If it didn't, it was on God's conscience. He made it blind.

The forty acres, once again, was up for grabs. It will be at least seventy to one in Court, Jerry predicted. " Who's got a sleeve with anything up it?"

Chapter Seven

'Mosie Takes No Prisoners.'

" Rommel, I read your book !" Moses turned over in his sleep, throwing off the covers he shared with Morty .

" You're having a nightmare, little fellow. Here, here's a hug. Go back to sleep. It's too early to get up." Morty put Mosie on his side and covered him again. His pet had been having more than a few of these troubled nights as the drama over the forty acres drew close to the end. His days had changed, too. He spent more time walking the land, often with Fritz, marking notes on a land map which the German shepherd had found in the Police headquarters. He was preoccupied .He was not easily distracted from whatever was occupying his thoughts.

His problem was a simple one. *Warfield Developments* always ended their campaigns with a devastating one-two punch. While exhausting the city with a costly and drawn-out legal battle, they would simultaneously mount a quick and aggressive stab at seizing the land outright. It left the city reeling from the unexpected prospect of fighting *Warfield* in a two-front war, something General Joel could have warned them was unsound .'Where', 'how' and 'when' had increased the poodle's anxiety. 'How' was the massive collection of steel, rubber, and glass riding on wheels and treads waiting for deployment in a nearby staging ground . 'Where' was *Second Chance* acres. ' *When'* was the enigma.

Moses did not ask the Conference to approve his Plan . He was the leader, the General. Nobody even considered raising a paw in objection. More important, the details were for 'need to know only'. He immediately chose Friedrich as his deputy, his consigliere. They settled on the tactical maneuvers to counter the coming onslaught .

The key to a victorious defense, Moses decided, was information, The dogs had to be swifter and sharper than the men opposing them. Used properly, it was as valuable as an armored division.

" Whippets and greyhounds," he ordered Fritz. " Round them up. Too bad, we don't have ocelots and jaguars roaming around to use. Let's call a come-to-

Jesus meeting to finalize plans."

The pets lined up and waited for orders. " We don't have enough messengers . You will do double duty. You will go in pairs, like a relay. Stick with the enemy .Let me know what he is doing... immediately. Don't run . Race! I need information.... in real time! Then go back to observe. Your buddy does the next run. Okay? Fritz will give you your stations. Good luck and don't break a leg."

Next were the dachshunds. " We have only four of you. That's bad. We really need eight. You will have to be in two places at once. Listen up. Just follow our instructions. Get to your assigned spots and wait. Don't worry about the first encounter. We anticipate what they will do. You will be protected. We've got your back."

The ' we 've ' referred to a group of Pit Bulls and Rottweilers. " You are as close to a tank group as we have. At the onset, you are going to be defensive, not offensive. That'll be a change for you, but trust me. Then, you attack. Take no prisoners . You stick with the Dachs. You are responsible for their lives."

Moses went on and on, instructing each group where they fit into the overall Plan, like pieces in a jigsaw puzzle. He knew where each dog was to be placed. He had surveyed the terrain like Publius Cornelius Scipio Africanus walking the Plains at Zama near Carthage before crushing Hannibal .They rehearsed over and over again until their movements were automatic.

Moses had other things to worry about. It had rained for three days making the roads muck and mud . Then, like magic, the sun came out and dried the ground.

" Now, " he pleaded one morning. " Now, Fritz. Please let them start today. We will finish them off !"

*. *. *. *. *.

As hoped for, the day began with glorious weather. It was 4:00 a.m. when Moses heard scratching at the back door. It was Fritz, out of breath. " I thought I'd better tell you. The Patrols are already out. Something big is going on. I heard them alert the big guns."

Moses grabbed a leftover *Pop*-Tart " I hope so.

We can't keep rehearsing the troops. It'll break their morale."

They had barely reached the highest mound on the field, when the first messenger arrived, without a hair out of place. " They've left the quarry and are heading here." '**Here**' was the key to victory or defeat! Moses had Plan A and a back-up Plan B and only minutes to decide between them. Information! Where was that damn dog? The first Whippet had no sooner taken off when his partner showed up.

There were two roads the machinery could take to reach the forty acres.. One led to the driveway next to Morty's house, The other, to the only abutter to give *Warfield* permission to cross her land. Mrs. Belasco did not like pets on the field; they were too noisy, she explained . She did yearn for a hair parlor within walking distance. *Warfield* promised her two.

" They are heading directly to Morty's driveway," the messenger repeated and raced back to the column of vehicles. Morty gave a sigh of relief. The enemy was doing exactly what he predicted they would do. Now, he had confirmation.

" Okay, Fritz. You know what's next . Fast!. Fast!"

The lead tractor started up the driveway, then,

suddenly stopped. The driver stood up and peered over the windshield. The four dachsunds, each about thirty inches long, were lying across the road, head to tail, stretching from one oak tree to its twin on the other side. They were apparently sleeping, tummies up, happy to be resting in the sunlight. Their owners sat in aluminum folding chairs watching them, some snoozing along with their pets.

Motors turned off, the drivers, comforted with the tranquil scene, leapt down from their running boards. They hurried to remove the furry nuisances and get on with their job. They did not even reach the first dach when the Rottweilers and pit bulls, hidden behind the seated ladies, rushed at them, snarling, teeth dripping saliva, eyes fierce and bloodshot. The tore at pants and cuffs and socks. They jumped up to rip jackets.They chewed at arms trying to shoo them away.

To show their support, the dachs set up a barrage of yelps and cries, high above their decibel punching weight. The unequal fight went on until the drivers decided that hourly union wages did not compensate for such hostility, especially when snapping jaws started aiming higher than knee caps.

Someone must have called a higher-up and sent

photos of the carnage because the column revved up again, motors grinding. This time, the equipment in the rear started to move in reverse. One after another, the machines retreated back into the town road, noses pointing back the way they had come earlier.

"Fritz, " Moses motioned for him to come closer. " Find out where they are going. If they are turning to the north entrance, tell the dachs and rotts to move to the Belasco entrance. I wish I didn't have to make them work again, but I need them all for....." Friedrich was off and running.

The greyhounds reported in every few minutes. As predicted, the column turned to the northern entrance. Just In time, the canine roadblock was reconstituted. The stand-off was the same, except it was the only accommodating abutter left to *Warfield* . It was too late in the day to try the Haberman driveway again. The team was under the gun. They had to hurry. The sky was getting dark. Wind rustled the leaves and bent the tall grass stalks. A few raindrops spattered down. There was not going to be any overtime for the *Warfield* work crew.

Moses hopped up Santa's broad back and dug his paws into the thick fur for safety. " Let's go, buddy. It's time for the kill! " Before leaving , he whispered something in the German Shepherd's ear. Fritz knew exactly what he must do. He waited until all the messengers had come in. They sat down on their haunches for orders.

"We've been over this. Find every dog. Get them to Belasco's. Split them into two columns. Half on one side of the road, the rest on the other side. Position them next to the markers, the pieces of yellow cardboard we put down earlier outlining both sides of the path for the tractors. If we have a downpour, you should be able to make out the markers for at least another hour. Remove the dachs' road block once all the machines have arrived and are in the road past the gate. We want the drivers to move forward in a tight group . Wave a few flags, Throw some flowers. Give them a kiss. Just get them all inside the fence."

The drivers could not believe it when the Dachshunds and Rottweilers moved to the sides of the Belasco driveway, clearing the way. It was uncanny. They were joined by all the other dogs in the field, large, small, white, black, mosaic. All barking and jumping up and down to show their enthusiasm for the invaders. The commotion and approaching dusk made it difficult to see where they were going. The column just followed blindly, one after other, the first tractor leading like the Pied Piper of Hamlin. The road slowly curved to the left....without notice.

Moses watched. He saw one group of beagles trying to straighten the path and eliminate the bend. He sent a Whippet to warn them to stop and follow the original plan. The drivers couldn't wait to park their vehicles in the field for the night and get home for some food and a leg over. Happy to be finished for the day, they shut off their motors and prepared to leave when they saw Moses approach. He stood up on Santa's back, thrilled by the sight. It was about to be a total slaughter!

" **One**," he called to his Deputy. Fritz shouted "'One' to the trio of Blues who howled out as if they were collecting an escaping group of sheep. The entire horde of dogs swept around the vehicles making a tight three-dog deep circle.

" **Two**". There was quiet as wheels began to sink into the marsh. No one had noticed the bog covered with day-flowers and grass. Pressing down with hundreds of thousands of pounds of steel, the machinery slowly, almost imperceptibly, sank into the spongy soil . All of them, within minutes, like boats in a retreating tide, lowered down to their running boards. The scene resembled an abandoned junk yard.

" **Three**." The drivers saw what was happening They tried to leap off to find higher ground. Santa and several other dense haired dogs picked up some large branches. They began to beat them against a group of poplar trees. The trees were not interested in playing games, but the hanging wasp hives were. The angry insects streamed out, ignoring the pets for the fleshy sweaty skins of the drivers. The men flung their hands and arms about to ward them away with little success.

" **Four**". The little dogs, the beagles, the terriers, the yorkies, the corgis, jumped on the vehicles and seized the water bottles, keys, food bags, lunch pails, backpacks, cellphones and dragged them into the muck.

" **Five!**" Moses was past compassion, sympathy, understanding. He was angry. He was violent. The early years of abuse and torture tore through him lacerating his core being. He felt the straps, the chains, the hunger, the kicks, the cold, the heat, the hell that humans had inflicted on him. He raged! He cursed, howling to the dog gods of revenge!.

"**Five**", he screamed again. Somewhere, concealed in the shadows, a dog jumped onto the back of another dog and rubbed his nose against a light switch. Powerful flood lights suddenly lacerated the darkness as cloud after cloud of hungry flies and mosquitoes dove down on the drivers, piercing their skin with biting, blood-sucking pain. The men fell .They desperately crawled for relief into the mud, made more filthy by their own shit and piss.

Not until the sun and morning coolness released them from their agony, did Moses leave. It was only a battle and not the war. Moses had no more tricks up his sleeves. He felt the weariness and satisfaction of a warrior. His sleep was sweet and untroubled.

Chapter Eight

'Mosie Triumphs over Evil'

Morty slid into the seat next to Jerry Hermann just as the judge was entering the Chamber. Everybody stood up. Everybody sat down. The *Warfield* table was thick with lawyers. They took over the first and second row of the Spectators' Section. They spent most of the time passing notes among themselves and leaning forward to hear what was going on. Nothing very substantial was.

Morty noticed that every other minute Jerry was jumping to his feet, objecting at something, waving files at every defendant testifying that *Second Chance* be opened for development. All morning, the identical scene played over and over. Even the Judge was losing his calm.

" What are you doing?" Morty asked.

" Really nothing. Just wasting time. Hoping these *Warfield* executives might accidentally spill something we can use."

" Does that ever work?"

" Occasionally. So far, not with these Shylocks. Marshall buys only the best." He suddenly broke off his explanation and jumped to his feet again.

*. *. *. *. *.

Moses slept well after his strategic triumph. By morning, he had forgotten his rage of the night before. He was not at ease. Something nagged at him before he fell asleep. It was waiting for him when he woke up. He could not identify the irritant nor the time nor place when it got stuck in his mind. He could almost hear the words blurred in the lost memory. It did not get clearer. It was something he had filed away long ago. Why he had done this was no clearer to him than what was stored.

He ate the breakfast Morty had left for him. He

did his ablutions as usual. Nothing wrong there. What was it? If he could just remember, he was certain it would help their case.

The feeling got stronger and stronger until with a sudden insight he knew what it was. Excited, he had to get to the Courthouse and alert Jerry. The lawyer could decide it was worthless, or valuable. Mosie had to let him decide. He had an intuitive feeling that it was critical to help their case.

Lawyers need evidence. He had heard that term often enough listening to conversations between the lawyer and Morty. He knew what the missing evidence was.

He climbed up on Morty's desk and riffled through the rat's nest of papers, *Pepsi* cans, books, pens, half empty coffee cups, envelopes until he located it. He jumped down, the letter clenched tight in his jaws. He looked at the clock. The Court would soon recess for lunch . What would happen when they returned was uncertain? Best to get there now. He bolted through the door and raced to meet the downtown bus. The driver saw the poodle running to catch up with him. He slowed down so they could meet at the next stop.

" Hop on, little man."

Mosie let the driver give him a tummy rub. He settled himself by his feet and impatiently counted off the stops . At the Courthouse, Moses jumped off and dashed to the rear of the building. No sense trying to go through the front door, not with the large forbidding 'No Pets' sign and watchful guards. There was a large truck parked near a loading platform in the rear of the building. Boxes of files were being wheeled out to be shredded. Moses slipped in without being noticed. Where was Jerry?

Skipping the first floor where administrative offices were located, he bounded up the back stairs, envelope still clenched firmly in his mouth. Now, which chamber?

There was a guard at each end of the corridor. The bustle of people coming and going hid him at first. Discovered, both guards moved to trap him. He had just enough time to push open the first door to a murder trial. No luck. At the second door a witness was leaving the *Warfield* trial. He swerved around her feet, almost causing her to fall . He entered the second Chamber on the run.

Bingo! There was Jerry on his feet and Morty

sitting morosely next to him with his head in his hands. Moses did not wait for formal introductions. He headed straight for the lawyer, screeching to a stop by his side, with the two angry guards fast on his heels. The Judge banged his gavel to quiet the noise. Mosie lifted his head to offer the envelope. He whispered, " you know what to do with this. Break a leg!"

Satisfied, Moses waited there, uncaring who grabbed him and tossed him outside. The bus ride home was pleasant. Moses, all relaxed, looked out the window, counting the telephone poles until the bus reached his stop. He had done his duty. Now it was up to the gold covered blind lady on the roof.

* *. *. *. *

Jerry did not need more than given a cursory glance at the paper Moses had brought. He approached the bench.

" Your honor, with your indulgence, I would like to place this letter in evidence. " He handed the letter to the Judge. " There should be no objection from

Warfield counsel. It is their document, signed by Mr. M.K.Warfield himself. "

The Judge handed the letter to the *Warfield* attorney . He read it, returned it. " No objection". Jerry then asked for a ten minute recess for his secretary to leave the courtroom and get something for him. Delighted with the opportunity to empty his bladder, the Judge readily agreed. Morty was totally confused at this point. Jerry did not say a word, until the secretary returned and handed him what he had sent her out for."

Jerry approached the Warfield executive who had been waiting, fidgeting in his seat all this time. He examined the new evidence.

" Do you recognize this letter?"

" I do. It is a form letter we send to all abutters when we are interested in obtaining a particular parcel of land."

" That is Marshall Warfield's signature?"

" It is."

" You have read the letter? You agree that the contents are accurate?"

" I do."

" Upon risk of perjuring yourself, you agree that

the contents are accurate?" He repeated again.

Hearing the word 'perjure', the executive was shaken. What was this Jewish lawyer driving at? Was there a trap somewhere on the page? He looked anxiously at his companions who were buzzing around in the bleachers. All nodded that the document was accurate, that they had idea of what Hermann was up to.

" I do"

" Let's put the letter aside… for the moment" He placed it ceremoniously on table.

" Now, please examine this paper. It is the one my secretary just brought in."

The witness looked at it as if it were some ancient Celtic incantation. " Okay " .He tried to return it.

" No, please hold it. We aren't finished with it yet. We will come back to the first in a minute."

The Courtroom quieted. The audience seemed prepared to have a rabbit jump out of a hat at any minute.

" Do you know who printed it?

" The government. The Postoffice."

" Do you have any reason to doubt its legitimacy?"

" None what so ever, " he replied." I've seen dozens of these."

" Maybe even hundreds?

" Yes. Possibly."

"Maybe even thousands?

" It's possible, but to that I can't be certain as you hold perjury over my head." There was a twitter from the Warfield contingent.

Jerry gave a gracious nod to his opponents. " Fair enough. For those in the audience, would you please explain what it is."

" To make sure that a letter is received after it is posted, this notice is attached to the envelope. When delivered, it has to be accepted and signed for. The receipt, with appropriate signature, is returned to sender as certified proof of delivery."

" Very good. Very sharp and clear. Nothing less than I would expect from a *Warfield* attorney. Now", holding up the first document, " these letters, the ones signed by Mr. Warfield, seventeen in all in this case, were sent to each abutter as legally mandated."

"Yes."

" Do you know why these seventeen had to be sent?"

" I do. In this city , to petition for a zone change, the municipal statutes required that each abutter to the parcel must be notified within a certain number of days, by certified mail, of the pending action."

" Very good." He smiled graciously. " That was done here? In this case?"

" Absolutely."

" You are certain?"

" Absolutely.

" Religiously and legally?"

" Legally yes. Religiously, I am not so certain. There is separation of Church and State in this country, Mr. Hermann. You should be aware of the First Amendment to our Constitution."

" True. Though I suspect each of the eleven billion dollar bills your earthly boss owns has ' In God we Trust,' stamped on it."

" Mr. Hermann, you are so smart I think we should recruit you for our side. " The remark was gratuitous and smarmy. The Judge started to object to the tone of the comment, but Jerry signaled,' forget it.'

" Thank you for the compliment. " He paused. " Would you please deliver to the Court the Certified notices returned to you as evidence you have followed the law? All seventeen of them."

" Of course....." He stopped as he saw the frantic waving and head shaking from his side of the room.

" Is there a problem? It is a simple request. You do not challenge the United States Post Office. The Court merely requests seventeen little pieces of paper. According to my secretary, it costs an extra five dollars and twenty cents each above the first class postage stamp Eighty eight dollars and forty cents to a company who counts its God given dollars in the billions. Five dollars and twenty cents to each of seventeen good citizens who surround a potential bonanza of millions."He turned to the judge for a judicial conformation. " Of course, to a man like Marshall Warfield who fires his executives if they do not straighten a crooked paperclip for its passage through eternity, that is sufficient enough expense to cancel a promised Thanksgiving turkey or Christmas ham."

"Yes. I would like to see the evidence also,"the Judge added.

" You wonderful little furry son-of-a bitch," Morty said out loud, though nobody was listening through the pandemonium which followed *Warfield's* admission they did not have the required tags, admitting they might be subject to perjury , to using the United States mail to defraud, along with a variety of other violations, all liable for severe monetary damages and criminal charges .

The noise ended with the Judge banging his gavel. A formal closing was mandated. It began with the judge pointing the handle of his gavel threateningly at the Warfield attorneys.

"I have sat here for two weeks listening as Warfield Developments has tried to deprive an honest charitable man out of his inherited family land. He made it plainly evident, early in this process, that he did not want to sell . You offered him more money than he could dream of in many lifetimes. He turned down every offer.

" You started an expensive legal campaign against him to force sale of the property.

" You authorized a brutal attack on the land itself, hoping to seize it before the shock had worn off.

" I declare your petition to set aside the designation of ' farming' as without moral nor legal merit.

" Moreover, I declare a year and a day

moratorium on attempts to obtain the land in question. I hope that during this cooling off period Warfield will realize the excessive cost to them in goodwill and fiscal liability and consider a wise decision to fold their tents and move elsewhere.

"I so move."

The gavel went down one final time.

As the occupants scurried for the exits, the Judge opened the door to his private office. Without even thinking if anyone was behind him, he stripped off his black robe, tossed it on a chair, dropped to the floor, turned over over onto his back, stretched out his hands and received the grateful hugs and wet kisses of David and Jonathan, his tiny gracious pure white Bichôns.

* *. *. *. *.

The debriefing took place at a nearby bar, lubricated by *Hassenfeffer* Lager .

" Let me tell you a story, Morty."

Four inquiring ears listened, Moses having waited next to a kind guard until he saw his two friends emerge.

" H.G.Wells, in the early nineteen hundreds, wrote a book called, *The War of the Worlds.* He was the fellow who wrote *The Invisible Man*. It takes place in England not too long ago. Out of the sky one day, drop huge spaceships. They release terrifying gigantic monsters, made of steel, which roam the countryside . Fire pours out of their weapons, killing everything in their way. They crush houses and buildings. The people ,the scientists, can do nothing to stop them. Army, rockets , bombs ,are worthless. Civilization is on the verge of total destruction.

" Then, a miracle happens. Suddenly the monsters falter and drop to the ground, lifeless. When they open up the massive steel casing, they find inside a small weak, pale person controlling the mechanical apparatus. When they examine the body, it has died of an ordinary bacterial infection, something we would pass off as a mild cold.

" Wells points out that God, in his wisdom, put on earth tiny insignificant forms of life destined to save the lives of his most wonderful creature , Man.

"Who would have thought that a few tiny pieces of paper have saved *Second Chance* for his most wonderful of creations, our furry friends."

" Hear! Hear! " Mosie was starting to slur his speech. " How about another?"

Instead, he was was treated to a round of head rubs, tummy rubs and a high-on-the shoulder burping. It wasn't fair, especially to one who had saved the world.

Chapter Nine

'Morty learns how to liase'

Although the ritual had taken place every ten years, give or take a year when some national emergency or epidemic had prevented it, this was the first time Morty was involved. Ten years, in this time and age, were like the swift passage of *Halley's Comet.* Both were eagerly anticipated. Both left a memory which decayed in a blink of an eye. The High School Class Reunion had arrived

The Posters tacked up in the hallways , reminding the students of its approach, made Morty pause more than once. His class year was included in the festivities to come. He was an alumnus. Students currently enrolled in classes, were not officially alumni, but in view of the chaos to take place in their confiscated classrooms, it was considered only fair to invite them to daytime activities and ship them home when the sun went down, letting their parents monitor their nighttime recreation.

Morty's involvement started with a handwritten note dropped into his message box. ' Please come see me Friday after the bell.... Aaron '. Aaron Luebbermann was the Principal of the James Buchanan High School. He had had been there a long time. ' Too long,' he complained to the School Board of which he was an ex- officio member.

" Jesus Christ," he would swear when the issue of special expensive tutoring for pregnant girls routinely came up. " I've been here so long I remember when condoms were called ' rubbers' and ' rubbers' were called 'prophylactics'.This off-color comment usually evoked the perpetual rejoinder from the only doctor on the Board, " Aaron, I'll bet you remember when you used sheep cecums?"

" Ah, those were the days, " The principal, his involvement no long needed, would slide his body down the seat and doze off.

Luebbermann was at least six feet four inches tall, thin with a determined look, like an emaciated bulldog. He would have been a perfect star on the high school basketball team were it not for his extreme whiteness, and his peculiar way of walking. He looked as if his top half was running away from his bottom half which lagged along at a slower pace. His nickname 'road runner', was introduced by a transfer student from Tucson. Unfortunately, it stuck. His lips were always pursed, his eyes hidden between steel-framed thick lenses. He never married and was proud of it.

" Ah, Mr. Haberman," he stuck his hand out and pumped furiously. " Good to see you. Yessseree. We forget how much we owe you for the smooth running of this citadel of learning. Can I offer you something? Perhaps a bottle of water? No? " He leaned back in his chair, tucked his feet up and gave a few swivels. " Yessseree". His eyes closed and his head slumped forward on his chest. He was asleep before the chair came to rest.

Morty wasn't sure what to do. The door opened and the secretary came in. She handed the bottle of water to Morty. " He does this often, these days. It's his circadian rhythm. When it gets quiet in here, I know he's in it again. Mr. Luebbermann!"
She shook him vigorously. " Aaron, wake up!"

Recovery was almost instantaneous. He was totally unaware of what had happened. " Yessseree. Do you agree? Do you accept?"

"What do I accept? Mr. Luebbermann? Please." He stopped the new round of swiveling.

" Ah, yes, Haberman. You know we are on next month for the tenth reunion. Would you loan us the use of your animal pasture? It would involve some tents, for about two days. We would take good care and put everything right at the end."

" Of course, Mr. Luebbermann. Aaron! ," Morty pleaded. " Stay awake. It's always been held in the school auditorium ."

" Please, stop shouting at me. Yes, it has been up to now. This year it's going to be different. Saint Catherine High School's reunion comes up the same time. The School Board thought it would be a nice gesture to invite them to join us."

"Isn't Saint Catherine the Catholic Convent? Are we going to mix with the nuns?"

" Oh, no, Morton.That would offend God. The Church also runs a high school for girls."

" You are going to have the girls from Saint Catherine and the boys from James Buchanan together? Both sets of returning alumni at the same time?"

" Why not? You can see why our auditorium will be

too small. What do you think? "

" I have no problem with it. The only thing is where are my pets going to play? I can't keep them cooped up in their cages ."

" Could they use our school yard? It's not as big as your field . What do you think?"

" Could work."

Morty watched the eyelids closing. They looked enormous under the far-sighted lenses.

" Okay...It's fine. Let's do it then....."

The arms of Morpheus had already reached up and gently dragged the principal down to sweet oblivion. On his way out, Morty stopped by the secretary's desk to tell her what had transpired.

" No need, Morty, I always keep the intercom on. It should be a hoot. I will let you know who you liaise with at Saint Catherine's ."

On the way home that afternoon, Morty started to realize the enormity of what he had agreed to. Nothing in his twenty eight years had prepared him for such responsibility. Maybe he was too hasty. He needed to talk with Moses. What did ' liaise ' mean? Was it some Catholic ceremony he would have to participate in? He was a good Jewish boy with a Bar Mitzvah he remembered well, and a circumcision he remembered not at all. If it meant converting, or some other Roman rite, he would withdraw his offer. On the other hand, if it was some inter-religion mating act, he would have to ask Mosie's advice.He did want his soul to remain pure, if not his body or discreetly selected parts of it. Morty was growing up. Was this all the 'fun and games' he was warned old age was about? Seemed rather timid and boring.

*. *. *. *.

Morty drove slowly. He was in no hurry to meet his contact at Saint Catherine's. Suddenly, Moses yelled out loud, " Stop! Stop the car!" The car screeched to a halt at the Police Station, gave a quick rattle and slowly relaxed. Moses jumped out, searched for the German Shepherd and came back.

" What was that all about? What was so urgent

with Fritz ?"

" You hear all these horror stories of people being lost in the woods or mountain climbing. Why you should always leave information where you are going ."

"We are just going to a girls' high school in the next town. What do you think is going to happen to us?"

" I don't know, but it's better to be safe than sorry. If we don't return, Fritz will know who were the last to see us alive ."

" Eat a *Slim Jim* and go to sleep."

"Morty, I have a bad feeling about this place."

" Why? It's just a high school like any other high school."

" No. It isn't. It's a Catholic high school."

" So? " he chuckled. He teased his poodle." Are you worried that they are going to burn you at the stake?"

" Are they going to burn me at the stake? Morty, remember who they did burn at the stake? It sure wasn't Catholics. It was the heretic Jews and Protestants. You are Jewish and I am a good Baptist. Wait until they call the local hardware store for some additional firewood and ask for us to deliver it in person and that's the last anyone ever sees of us, firewood and all. "

" You know all this for sure?"

" Any group that goes around saying that you are killing little Catholic babies and using their blood for Passover matzoh must be hiding something. You just don't come up with a bizarre accusation like that out of the blue. I'll bet it comes from some secret Vatican catechism. "

" Mosie, quiet down. Please don't talk about your black masses . We are almost there." The wide wrought iron gates were pulled back. The guards waved a merry salute, all smiles and of cheer.

Moses responded with a muffled curse, "Probably programmed to do that, to keep us off our guard, like the orchestras playing music at the entrance to the concentration camps. You know I'm not reneging on your offer, but I just wanted you to know. I have a responsibility to protect you."

Morty ignored him. Maybe it's the dogfood I'm feeding him he wondered.

Morty parked the car in the visitors' section. A young female student, dressed in the school uniform, dark blue jacket, white blouse, tie and pleated skirt, came up to them, gave a little bow, and said sweetly " Welcome to Saint Catherine's. Can I help you?"

Moses gave a hostile bark. He whispered, " See. It starts already. We're not even inside yet."

' Moses, be quiet. She can hear you."

" I doubt it. They are programmed only to hear the screams of the tortured."

" Moses, I think you are being para...para.... You are getting me to forget that word you taught me."

" The word is ' paranoid'. You are using it correctly. Kudos to you, kid. Let's go in. Remember, keep your back to the wall, and you refuse to visit their shower bunker."

*. *. *. *.

The Headmaster's office was an attractive room, more like a living room than an administrative one. Comfortable furniture and floor lamps. Not a fluorescent bulb in sight.

" I am Sister Teresa. I understand we will be working with you to plan for the Reunion. We are all very excited." She bent down holding her hand out to Moses. This was not easy effort as rolls of love handles blocked her repeated attempt. There was really no place for Sister Teresa to go, as the belly rolls had already claimed territory on her face and chins. What went on under the habit was anyone's guess….. not really.

" This is Moses? I am glad you brought him. 'Out of the bulrushes' is he? The noble Egyptian prince who dedicated his life to liberate an oppressed people? How proud he must be. A beacon of hope."

Moses felt an immediate attraction to the nun. How could he hide the treason from Morty?

She stood up," Don't let me waste your time. I'm sure it is not me you traveled to see . Let's go find Izzy for you."

'Izzy?' 'Isidore'? ' Issac'? The afternoon was full of surprises. What possibly could be next?

The Conference Room was a corner room, situated to receive the fragrant breezes of the garden from windows on both sides. It was impossible not to recognize the dense scent of lilacs . The day was hot. Rectangles and squares of sunlight poured through the windows, unopposed by curtains or blinds. They etched hot golden patterns on walls and skin.

Standing in front of an open window, was a young

girl. Her cotton shift was moving forward and back as the wind entered and retreated . She was short, thin, possibly five four or five with the mature fulness of a young woman . Her hair was a pure black, parted in the center, collected into two rivers of braids. Her skin was a light olive, clear complexion . Her eyes were large with dark pupils, which made one remember the legend of belladonna . Her lips were drawn back, revealing white teeth which fluttered like butterflies when she talked.Her fingers were long and slender They seemed to move with the breeze.

She was beautiful, even stunning. Her parents were proud of her beauty. Her two older brothers were proud of her beauty. Anyone who met her was captured by her beauty. Even the German Shepherd by her side was proud of his mistress's beauty.

The only one who was unaware and could never in her lifetime appreciate what God or Nature had bestowed upon her, was the maiden herself. She had never seen her image. She lived in a cold colorless private world where ' beauty' and 'ugliness' were just vacant, empty words, like 'blue' or 'yellow' or 'hazy' or 'clear', without substance or nuance. Isabella had been born blind, though with the best of intentions.

If ever Moses was at a loss as how to greet a stranger, this was it. Did he shake her hand? Did he guide her hand to his? What about taking it and giving it a kiss?Wasn't that a little too formal for today? What about giving her a hug? Was that too familiar, especially with the pudgy guardian in the room? Back to the kiss? That could be the height of folly. It couldn't be on her lips, despite the attractiveness of the idea . Should he kiss her on the cheek? Which cheek? What about the other cheek? And back again? How could saying a simple 'hello' be so difficult?

The solution was provided by Isabella herself. She stretched out her hand. " Just shake it, Mister Haberman. It will stand the shock and we will be good." Was that a joke? She barely knew him.

That was the other surprise. Her voice was deep, like a man's, full powered, resonant and vibrant.There was a vocal thrill like a bass chord drawn slowly from a viola or oboe. It was a good-natured voice with cadence rising at the end of each sentence. Where did it come from?

" You can drop it now, the hand, Mister Haberman. It pays my salary here at Saint Catherine's. You can't have it for nothing." She was teasing him, even while staring at him with blank eyes. He dropped the hand. She had gotten inside him. He could not tell how or where, but there was a hole in his body, the faintest of penetrations. He was possessed. He wanted nothing more than to scoop her up , squeeze her to death. To be her protector the rest of his life.

" Let's do it, " she ordered. He considered for an moment she had heard his thoughts and was giving permission. It was unlikely.

" You'll have to drive, though, until we get away from the school. Then we change seats. I hope you don't mind fast drivers. I've had most experience driving at night without the moon. It makes us all equal." She laughed.

A ripple of teasing started again deep in her chest then rumbled up and down her body. He could have fun with her. Not the kind he had with Mosie, rolling around on the floor and giving belly rubs. A different kind, but he'd be damned if he knew what it was. Something that twenty eight ears of life had not prepared him for. He was aware that she knew exactly what that was. It was a very scary thought.

" My name is Isabella Cordelia Quiros. I have two older twin brothers, Damon and Pythias. I like to be called Izzy. My brothers like to be called Damie and Pithy. Please don't mix them up. My brothers would never know what to do if you call them 'Izzy'. They are very insecure about their sexual identity, something I have no problem with. You are free to call me Damie or Pithy if you prefer. I really believe I am a female, so I'm in a safe place if you are confused. What about you? You're convinced you are a male? So many people go around here not knowing if they are male or female. It must make sexual intercourse rather complicated? Don't you think?"

The words buzzed around him like excited bumblebees. The words themselves were familiar but why didn't they settle down for a minute and let him put them in order?

" Don't worry, Mr. Haberman . We'll have plenty of time to sort out your sexual disorientation. Typical young male confusion."

She didn't stop. He didn't want her to stop. It was like a musical melody which swam around and around , out of reach, never quite reaching the shore.

'I think we should head out now, if we are going to walk the field and get back in time for the School to feed me, unless you think I am too fat and should be locked up when food is around."

" No.. no... you can eat. I mean you're not too fat. Yes... I'll make sure we get back in time."

"Wonderful, she picked up his hand and shook it vigorously. " I am Mister Haberman, " she intoned seriously, " I live in Lisbon Hills. I am a custodian for the James Buchanan High school. I have a lovely castrated male toy poodle, named Moses. I have a grassy field of forty acres. There is a teacher at the Saint Catherine School whom I am going to escort to visit my field. Then, I am going to drive at twice the speed of sound to get her back for a dull, miserable dinner at the School unless she would prefer going out with me to *McDonalds* for a happy meal."

He was totally bewildered." Did I get it right, or did I leave something out?" It wasn't a bad idea .Why hadn't he had summoned the courage to suggest it on his own? Where did it come from?

Mosie was not quite as dense as poor Morty. " Ask her about her dog. That should give you time until you land on earth again."

It was a wise suggestion. The German Shepherd was an older, much more mature and disciplined than his age would suggest. The product of superb training by the F.B.I. Discarded when Federal funding dried up ,he had been seconded to the *Hartford Connecticut Academy of Seeing Eye Dogs.* It was an instant love fest when the blind lady from Ohio turned up. He would give his life for her and she would give her life for him. It was a match made in heaven.

" This is my friend, Newton."

" Ask her ' why Newton?" Morty was approaching earth, his rocket engines slowing down to achieve a nice soft memorable landing.

" You know about Issac Newton?" She asked.

"He was a famous English scientist. We studied him in Science class. He discovered light and gravity."

" Pretty close, Morty. I guess you didn't spend your school days looking at girls' breasts, like my two brothers?"

' God! Would she never stop? Morty was beginning to feel a strange sensation which, up to now, only happened when he was in bed after watching Mosie movies.

" Newton discovered that light was made of several lights, like the colors of the rainbow, and that gravity made apples fall down instead of up. He received many awards for his discoveries . At one of those dinners, he got up and said, ' If I have seen more and achieved more than others have, it is because I have stood on the shoulders of giants.' I feel the same way. Thanks to my Newton's shoulders, I can almost see the stars."

That was what he wanted to be. To be the 'shoulders' that would one day let her reach the stars. His mission was out there. He was convinced of success.

CHAPTER TEN

'Isabella Trumps Morty's Heart'

The afternoon passed quickly. *McDonald's* was packed as usual with students stoking up to avoid an institution dinner which was usually unexciting, tasteless and too abundant. Morty settled for fried chicken tenders, Moses for a naked hamburger without the bun and vegetables, and Isabella for a double 'everything' with additional ' everything ' on top of it.

Morty watched in awe as she deconstructed more calories than he consumed in a day.

" Do you have any brothers or sisters? " she asked between mouthfuls.

" I was an only child, at least that's what I was told. I was in foster care until I was six and then adopted. The family had no children. They treated me like their own. I was very fortunate. What about you?"

"You know about Damie and Pithy. My father had a shoe store in Costa Rica until the 'time of the gangs'."They looted and burned people they disliked;

our family was on their list."

" Why?"

" We were Protestant. It was a Catholic country."

" See, I told you, Morty." Moses kicked his leg. " They do that all over. That's the way they are. If they don't, they go to hell and are roasted for eternity in a big rotisserie.'

" Be quiet. That's not nice. She's a guest."

" That's when we came to the United States. It was't easy getting here, but we had friends here who helped."

" You don't mind working at the Convent ?"

" They were the 'friends' who helped. "

The conversation went back and forth. " You never had any sisters in any of the homes?"

" I wish I had. It would make it easier for me to talk to you."

" You're doing fine. I like your company "
She took a hand and stroked it between her's.

Morty grew red in the face. He began to speak, but the words got mixed up. He shifted in his seat, trying to get more comfortable, tugging on his crotch.

" Relax. " said, " You can't help it. The penis has a mind of it's own. We don't have such problems.

Probably advanced evolution."

' Penis?' Nice girls didn't use those words. Not even nice boys, at least most of the time. He had never said that word, except when he and Mosie were having a serious come-to-Jesus talk about sex.

" Morty, it's natural when someone has two older brothers . We used to sleep in the same room until my father noticed they were getting hair on their legs. I was banished to the little storage room off the kitchen. Not even a window. They were able to stay in the big room. It wasn't fair!"

" Your father was a wise man."

" I wanted to stay with them. I didn't want to change rooms. Damie and Pithy were lots of fun. They never did anything bad to me, though they were always joking around. Sometimes they would tease a little too far. My father would strap their ass.They treated me a like brother,,,,,until...." She stopped. How far should she go with this obvious virgin?"

" One day they blindfolded me. They got naked and asked if could tell which willy was whose. They had played the game with some of the girls in school. It was disgusting. I told them so. They laughed."

" Did you tell your parents?"

"Absolutely not. I took care of it in my own way."

" What did you do?"

" I peed in both of their beds and told my mother they were bed-wetters."

" My parents brought them to the doctor who gave them very unpleasant examinations. That was the end of that. They advanced to girls who gave them a longer run for their money than I did. It was fun watching them telephone for a date, getting dressed for one, and questioning their identical twin what they should do to get laid, which was usually a futile exercise. " She laughed. " It's too bad you never had a sister."

The conversation drifted. Morty felt the time had come to reveal a bit of what he was feeling.

" You're beautiful, Isabella." He kissed her on the cheek.

She shivered, clutching her arms around her. Her lips pursed to say something back, to deny it or thank him. No words came out. The tears did, one after another. Soon she was openly crying and no amount of tissues could hide it. She lowered her head to hide her embarrassment. She stumbled her way out of the restaurant." Take me home. Please, Morty. Drive me back. Thank you. It is not you. It is me. Don't ask why. You wouldn't understand Please take me home. Don't call me I 'll call you."

They rode home in silence, Isabella in the back seat, sobbing. Moses rode in front, on Morty's lap " It's not your fault, Morty." Moses tried to comfort. "You did nothing wrong. I will explain. Just drive carefully. You are weaving all over the place. I want to get back in one piece. Look at the road. Don't think of what happened. Isabella is okay. She will be fine. You are not responsible for this."

Morty had a cold supper. He prepared for bed but lingered in the living room. Instead, took a Hassenreffer and opened it. He took his finger and held it over the mouth. He tilted the bottle wetting his finger. He gave the taste to Moses who licked it off. A few more and it was Morty's turn.

" Well? You haven't said much, my friend, "Morty started the conversation.

Mosie was stumped. How can you describe the Northern lights or a rainbow to someone blind from birth?

" You told her something about herself that she does not understand. How is she to respond? Can she say, 'thank you. You are, too? You see the problem?"

" I think so."

" You are using words in our language which mean something only after they have passed through the filter of our five senses. Like ' noise', 'thunder', 'water dripping' . You need ears and eyes to process those words. You need skin to understand 'touch', a mouth to recognize ' sweet or salty.' Nature gave us those senses to help us to understand our world. Without them, we are a helpless drifting cell , or something even lower in the scale. If you were born without a nose, what would freshly mowed hay or lilacs mean?"

" What's the answer? I can't abandon her. If she weren't blind, she would have been snatched up by a man a long time ago. Don't you agree?"

'I do."

" It's only her blindness that scares men away. Don't you agree?

" I do, Morty. Honestly, I've never been in your predicament. I have no frame of reference for human love problems. Suppose you placed her hand into a flowing stream and said " I can't show you, but I will love you as long as this water flows to the sea. Or my love is as hot as the burning sun." He was getting excited, " My love is as solid as this rock, and so forth"

" They are all rather corny, Mosie."

" So is love. Romance is a mixture of hormones and enzymes, and biochemical reactions and altered blood flow. How would a lab experiment know what is corny or not?"

Regardless of whether a rock would know the difference between an ear of corn and an eclipse, both men slept a long peaceful sleep of the holy and virtuous.

The next morning, " Moses cautioned, " Let her do the talking. I'm certain it 's not the first time someone has said it to her. She is lovely. She doesn't know what that is. She can't see what you can. How can she tell if the person is sincere or lying?"

*. *. **. *. *.

" Please, Morty, don't get upset at what happened. I get emotional at things that you would find silly."

" No. No. " he interrupted, " It was okay. I

worried if I had said something to offend or hurt you."

" You didn't. It made me realize that I've never seen you. I would like to. Now, if it is alright with you"

Moses had said to wait for her to take the first step. It was good advice. He waited until her hand passed over his face. It was soft, as he would have expected, but the moistness and barely noticeable tremor weren't.

" You have large ears, Morty, " she said. " Are they something you were born with or were they surgically added ? They go very well with your nose and eyes. Yes. Wise choice. Don't leave home without them."

The light-hearted banter was just what Morty needed. She probably did go through experiences like this before.

" I will try, Izzy. However, they are not easy to attach. One day, before coffee, I put the ears on the wrong sides. I heard everything backwards that morning. Nobody had the courage to tell me. I never found out until I saw myself in the Men's Room mirror."

She laughed. " Good for you, Morty, I think you are joking with me." She pulled on his ears. " Good glue." She continued her inspection. All the anxiety and tension was gone. He actually took her fingers and let her run them through his hair.

" Please let me know if my toupe is on straight."

" I can't tell you that, but it seems to be on tight," she playfully tugged on his hair.

Her fingers were butterflies on his cheeks, his eyes, his lips. He took her hand and kissed it. There were no tears. She took his hand and kissed it back.

" Well," she joked. " The hard part's over. Now, you pick me up, take me to your lair and seduce me. Not here, the table's too hard. "

He could not tell whether she was still making fun of him. He did not object to the suggestion although the logistics had never filtered through any of his five senses.

" I think we should go. It's getting late."

They did not move. Morty got up and refreshed their coffee, along with the purchase of a lemon cake and two forks.

" How can you teach English Literature?"

" Technology helps. It wouldn't have been possible when I was born. I learned Braille years ago, but I use it so seldom I probably need a refresher course. Almost all books today are recorded so I can hear them. I have a little gadget that I run over the lines in a new book and a voice reads them back to me. My computer talks to me so I can 'read' a paper a student has submitted. I can criticize it and my voice is translated into words on his or her computer. I haven't had much trouble, so far."

Morty was reminded of how little he had done to get more education. Should he blame it on lack of determination or faulty genes?" I' m just a custodian, really a janitor, " he impulsively burst out, "I need you to know ."

" Morton Haberman! The only thing I didn't know about you was the size of your ears, and something else which we don't discuss in mixed company. I should tell you my secret. I like to swear, so don't get offended. Just take your ears off. My brothers used to swear all the time. When they cut themselves shaving, you could hear them curse down the street. I thought my father would be angry, but he would come upstairs, stand next to Pithy and add to the noise. I asked my mother why she said nothing. She told me the story of Mark Twain, the *Huckleberry Finn* guy. He used to swear horribly when he was shaving. One day, his wife repeated back the stream of curses. When she had finished, he said, " my dear, you have the words, but not the melody."

Isabella stood up, reached for Newton' harness. She leaned awkward across the table and whispered loud enough for the elderly couple in the next table to blush. " Let's get the fuck out of here, the doughnuts are for shit."

'Roll with the punch' , Mosie had advised. ' Let her do the talking.' No difficulty there, he promised himself. What in the world could he say to this complex package of challenging desirable Isabellas? He was a poorly educated, poorly paid janitor with big ears. What could he say? What could he offer?

Chapter Eleven

' Is love more than a rub on the ass?'

Isabella had an intuitive sense of where the Reunion activities were to take place on the field. She knew where the two tents were placed, the smaller one for food, drinks, snacks and a bulletin board to hold messages for returning alumnae. The larger one had a rows of collapsible chairs, a dance floor, speaker's platform and disco tables. Once they learned the secret from his secretary on how to keep the Principal awake, with caffeine rich expresso, the list of activities , indoor and outdoor was easily approved.

Despite their efforts, the Reunion schedule seemed stale and shopworn. It was the same itinerary that had been around for decades with minor technological improvements.

" I don't care for it , Morty. " Isabella complained. " No wow. No pizzazz. What would you say to some strippers for the men, and *Chippendales* for the ladies? Maybe a performance of 'The Full Monty ' to jazz things up?'"

Morty was getting weary of the whole business, too. However, exposing the maidens of Saint Catherine's to male genitalia might be a little too daring, especially with the nuns hovering about.

" I'm sure the men would love it," he chuckled . We could put a big sign up advertising the strippers as ' Exotic Cleopatras from the Mysteries of the Nile.' That should fool the nuns."

" Morty, not all of the nuns are virgins. Some of them have taken vows after being married and having children. It is a late-life choice for them. Many of the high school teachers are free-spirits like me. I think the Law would hustle you and your Egyptians off the premises. The men, as going by my brothers, would place bets on how long it would take to deflower a virgin."

" I didn't think strippers were virgins."

" For this shindig, they'd better be over the age of twelve."

" Okay," he agreed with a sigh. " Anything else ? I'm ready to call it a day. For a change, do you like Chinese food? There's a great place down by the river.'

" I don't know, Morty. Does it have an opium den?

I've read about places like that. Yellow men with one black pigtail , long mustaches wearing silk dresses."

" You've been seeing too many old black and white movies. This restaurant has good chow mein and egg rolls." He realized what he had said." I didn't mean to….."

She took his hand. " Morty, this won't be the first time you'll say something like that. If we see each other, see I am as guilty as you are, we will both make off-hand comments like that. It is a built-in way of our communicating with each other. Probably in our DNA by now. Forget it. We don't need to apologize every time. Let us agree to ignore it. Is that okay with you? It is with me."

It was an irrational act. It was a spontaneous act. It happened so quickly he didn't have time to realize what he was doing or what the consequences would be. He wrapped his arms around her and squeezed her to tell her he agreed. She reciprocated. For an instant , the original reason for the embrace was completely forgotten by the two of them.

Isabella was the first to speak. " That was nice, Morty, but you could have e-mailed me your answer. My computer talks to me."

" I prefer this, " he answered back. 'I hope you like we old fashioned guys. "

" I do, big ears and all. We'll tackle the activities list when I can count on your undivided attention. I can feel big things developing down below. Don't forget I lived with Damie and Pithy and know all about your male hormones."

It was too embarrassing to find an unembarrassing answer.

*. *. *. *.

" Well , Morty , let's go over the Agenda . Maybe you've come up with some more suggestions. In the morning, we have a breakfast for those who arrived the night before. They visit the classrooms where the students have put up art exhibits and science projects. Then lunch in the big tent, followed by Mr. Luebbermann's welcoming speech, 'How James Buchanan High School is the ever shining beacon for humanity, freedom and motherhood.' Free afternoon with sports in the field. To the motels to change. Cocktails and dinner in the big tent. Any entertainment we can schedule."

" Pretty dull so far, Morty," Moses disparaged.

" Wait. Wait." Morty added. " The dance with the student band is good. 'Golden Oldies', swing and rock. Something for every one. "

" More dull."

" At the close we are going to have a dog show. Those who live nearby will be encouraged to bring their pets. The rest will act as Judges. "

Moisie thought about it. " What, " he wondered, excited, "if you announced that this year, you were going to reverse the contest? Dogs run around the tent with their owners? It's not a contest for the ' best in show' dogs, but for their owners. Put the owners on all fours with a leash and have them trot around with their pets. The audience will vote for the human who is the ' best in show." He or she will get a tummy rub, a biscuit and a blue ribbon."

Enthusiastic over the idea, Morty added," We can award a second and third place ribbon for the winners."

"The yearbook photographer can take pictures and put them in them in the small tent for sale . Great idea, little man. I wish I could tell them where the idea came from. " He bent down, " you deserve a tummy rub for that."

" If it's all the same to you, I'd really prefer some *Fluff*."

" That leaves only one sore spot, Mrs. Belasco."

" I 'd love to know
what ails that lady. She still refuses to open her driveway to the field."

" You need permission for her access road. Remember what the Fire Chief warned. The Permit requires at least two entrances for the fire trucks to get in ." I wish somebody would knock that lady off."

Moses thumped his fist over his heart, knelt down and kissed Morty's hand, " Godfather, " he swore, in a solemn voice. " I will remove the pebble in your shoe. Just command me in all things!"

Morty laughed, " Moses, you've got to hit the sack earlier. You are watching too many Al Pacino movies."

Neither of them moved. Morty said in a low voice tone as possible, "She squeezed my ass."

" What did you say?'

" She squeezed my ass."

" She squeezed your ass ?!?"

" She did, and I squeezed her back."

" Oh my god ! Oh my god! We are in deep shit. First thing, tomorrow, we get you an AIDS test. Then a pregnancy test. Two pregnancy tests. You go into quarantine seclusion for fourteen days to rule out whatever you are incubating. You didn't do anything else? If you did, tell me. That's all?"

Morty looked as if he was going to have a panic attack at any moment.

" Is it dangerous to have your ass rubbed? I don' t know those things. Tell me, Moses, and be honest"

" It's okay. Did anything else happen?"

" She kissed me on the mouth."

" No. That tramp ! That hussy ! That strumpet!"

"Please, Mosie. Be serious. Did I do anything wrong? I don't want to do anything to make her not like me."

" Morty, you have nothing to worry about. She did everything first? You're sure? Did you kiss her back?"

" I had to. I had no choice I couldn't help myself. I don't know what happened. I had no control,"

" I"ll tell you exactly what happened. You are in

love."

" Is that what falling in love is? An ass rub? I don't know, Morty. Why was I so afraid of it all these years ? I do it to you all the time. Does that mean we have to get married?"

'Could be worse,' Moses mused. ' Thank God he doesn't know what else is coming. Poor guy..... at least hold off until the Reunion is over.'

*. *. *. *. *.

Mrs. Belasco had no chance to escape her destiny. Not when informed that that the *Homeowners Association of Abutters* had unanimously chosen her as Queen to represent them. The glittering gilded crown was brought along to show her. The scepter was festooned with man-made jewels, more sparkling than real ones. The fake fur ermine and satin robe was displayed along with swatches of fabric color for her to choose from. She gave in easily. Her protests that she had not changed her mind about the noise, but that she was a generous soul, produced such expressions of exuberant joy from her neighbors, that the good lady was already wondering about the next reunion.

*. *. *. *. *.

Morty and Isabella stood hand in hand by the exit to the field. The Reunion was an unqualified success. The compliments and accolades for their work swept over them. It was a moment of joy. The praises were for both as if they had merged into one.

Isabella was standing in her stocking feet. It had been a long day. Her feet were aching. Despite the cornucopia of food still uneaten in the large tent, she needed to relax first and put her feet up.

" Can we go to your house? I need to rest a bit and give you a hug.Thank you for your help. It was really great."

There were no objections from Morty. Even Moses was happy at the suggestion. He made his acceptance known by asking for some hugs. He anticipated an excellent possibility of being exiled by the pair later on. He was taking no chances.

Isabella stretched out on the sofa. She rubbed her

feet. Morty moved close and put his arms around her. Something still nagged at him. The BIG question had scrupulously been avoided by both of them. It needed to be asked and answered, once and for all.

" I think you know I love you. If you love me, why? It's beyond me. You could have anyone you want. I'm just me.... Not really anything. You have to tell me."

" Ah, the big talk. I knew that sooner or later mother would have to sit you down and explain the facts of life. " She curled up and brushed his face with her lips.

" If you are poor, you can find ways to make money. If you are uneducated, you can find a lot of ways to get educated. If you are short, you can wear high heeled shoes. If you are tall, you learn to slouch a little. If you are blind, like me, I can get artificial aids to compensate , to 'see' if you will.

" In this world, today, you can get practically anything you want, in one way or another. Not everything. Not perfect, but good enough. However, some things are so rare that there's precious little to go around. That's was makes it so sought after. So hard to find. So much to be desired.

" It is goodness. A rare grace which nature has

given to only certain privileged persons . I can't see you, Morty. Not with my eyes. I can only judge by your actions and my feelings. They tell me you are one of those persons. Someone I want to know more about. I love you, too." She stretched up to kiss him."I think it is time, Morton Haberman, that you and I have sexual intercourse."

Morty's mind was blank. Moses had instructed, ' don't think. Just go with the flow.'

Isabella took his hand and asked him to lead her to the bedroom." I don't want to disappoint you," she said. " I believe that you and I were meant to be together. It says so in the Bible. When Adam was lonely, he asked God for a companion. God said 'what about a woman?' Adam asked 'what is a woman?' God replied that it was a human being like Adam, only smaller, softer, kinder, compassionate, sensitive and sensual. God said they were expensive, even in the Garden of Eden. They cost an arm and a leg. Adam asked ' what can I get for a rib?' That's the story as told in the Book of Genesis."

She could not ignore that one last joke. " I guess I'm your missing bone. I predict, however, that before the night is over, you will have another lovely one to share with me. Our conjugal night should be full of surprises."

Later, still coupled in bed, comforted by Moses' steady snoring and occasional fart, Isabella was finally able to complete her vision of a good man.

CHAPTER TWELVE

'A deadly walk in the woods.'

Friday night was pizza night. Morty and Mosie shared a pepperoni, mozzarella, olive oil, garlic, onion, tomato, sausage, *King Kong* specialty. Isabella went for the pineapple, avocado, banana, pecan variety which forced her to eat her abomination separately in the kitchen with Newton.

" How can you eat that foul concoction ?" Morty asked, sautéed onion rings still on its way down to his lower bowels, after releasing its signature fragrance.

" Brush your teeth before you go, " Izzy advised, wiping her lips with a delicate touch.

The one good thing from Lavinia's brief encounter with Morty were the books she chose for the custodian. Morty was fascinated by the recent advances in heating and air conditioning systems. He resented the 1922 steam boiler in the basement of the school. He cursed at the thermometer which knew exactly when to shut down the heat on subzero days. He petitioned the School Board for a swap with modern heat pumps. With Isabella's urging, he signed up for an evening semester at the Community College to learn more. Tonight he was scheduled to trade garlic fumes for erudition.

"Why don't the three of us go out for a walk?" Isabella proposed after Morty left.

" The weather is a little wet. Are you sure?" Mosie worried.

" Do you know why I like to get outside on days like this?"

" Tell me why, pretty lady."

"I can see the seasons as well as you can."

" What's the trick?"

" There isn't any. Winter is no problem.. Cold. Snow. Ice. Bundle up in heavy clothes. Cars driving slow and skidding on ice. Fires in the living room. Free school days when stormy."

"Okay, I give you that one."

"Summer. Skimpy clothes. Hot. Mosquitoes. Sweat. Iced tea. Swimming. Long days "

" You've got that one, too."

"Spring and fall are trickier. They are the transition seasons. Part of one season and part of another. Fall is getting colder. Days you need a sweater. Nights you turn on the thermostat. Dry leaves crunching on the ground. New smells. Fire. Smoke. It happens to be my favorite season.

"Spring is simple. Sweaters come off. Outside without jacket. Air wet. Ice melts. Buds on branches Birds chirp again. Lilacs."

" Izzy, if that dumb lunk doesn't marry you, I will."

" Why not?" She paused. " Mosie, we can't ! Damn it !"

"What's the problem?"

" The laws on bestiality in this state are horrendous. They'd lock us up, or at least me. We wouldn't be able to see each other for years. Oh, Moses..." she squeezed him hard. " Will you wait for me? It shouldn't be more than twenty years, tops?

" As long as it takes, my darling. Now, let's hit the road."

The sun was setting. The ground fog , a hazy layer of cooler air, was settling over the warmer earth. The road was wet with a slippery layer of crushed dead leaves. The trio turned north onto a graveled road . Isabella could feel the change from a pavement.

" Where are you taking me, Mosie?"

" Not too long ago, this area was farmland . You can still smell the pasture. Builders with no souls are ruining it. Clusters of new houses surround the old ones which have not been forced out."

" What a shame."

" Did you bring any money?"

" Of course. A young lady never leaves the house without a twenty in case she is kidnapped and needs to buy her freedom."

" It probably won't cost that much. I thought we could drop in on Mrs. Lounder. You would like her."

" Tell me about her."

" Not a happy tale. Marilyn was in school with Morty. Attractive young lady. Unhappy home. Both parents alcoholic. Suspect she married to get out of an abusive situation. Donny Lounder was good-looking. Not too bright. Classmate of Morty's. They were friends. Donny and Marilyn got married. Had to. Marilyn was three months pregnant when Donny joined up, went to Iraq and was promptly killed."

" Sad. Sad.." Izzy said. " We forget what that war did."

"Donny 's pension was barely enough. Marilyn is good cook . She sells pies and cakes to local restaurants and to anyone traveling up this far. That's why I asked if you had some money on you. Marilyn would not charge us for two muffins, but she needs the money ."

" No problem, Mosie."

It was an old farmhouse. Moss patches growing on worn out black asphalt shingles which needed replacement years ago. White paint, peeling around decaying wooden window frames. Lopsided front steps. Scattered bicycles and toys on wannabe lawn.

A very happy eight or nine year old little boy waved from the porch. He jumped off and ran towards them, excited to have guests. When he got closer, he could see the lady and the two dogs. It was the dogs which made him so happy. He hadn't any pets. The visitors were an early Christmas gift delivered to his front door.

He raced closer, eyes fixed on the furry friends. He saw nothing else. Not even the white *Porsche 911 Carrara* convertible which burst out of nowhere headed directly towards him. Tires screeching, roaring recklessly, it smashed into him......and never stopped.

As far as Mosie could remember, Donny Jr. was not flung to the right or the left, or even over the roof of the car or under it. The body simply disintegrated, atom by atom, shedding all its DNA into the air, in a single second The driver, registering the two dogs, one wearing a leather chest harness, increased his speed, leaving behind as the only witnesses to the murder, one blind girl, one seeing- eye German Shepherd, and a talking poodle.

*. *. *. *.

" That's the whole story, Morty. It happened so fast, I have to stop and think."

" You are sure about the car?"

"Absolutely," Moses confirmed. " It was 'Chips' Gannon's. I watched you wash it enough times to be familiar with it. It was going fast. It never even tried to slow down to make the turn into our road. I could glimpse the two medallions he got from the 'Sierra Mountain Relay' he entered few years back They're two shiny metal insignias sticking up from his back license plate holder. I also bet it's the only white

Porsche 911around these parts."

" Was he alone in the car?"

" There was a woman in the passenger seat."

" Do you know who it was?"

" That's difficult to say. We were in the center of the road. The car comes barreling in on our right. She would have been in the passenger's seat. She had blonde hair, loose. That's really all I can remember."

" He didn't slow down or stop?"

"No."'

" Maybe he thought he had hit an animal or deer. He was in a hurry to get somewhere. It could have been a family dog . He wanted to avoid all the paperwork and tears."

" Possible. Remember, he did kill a child. He is murderer. He's free and still out there. We are the only witnesses and we can't say anything.

" Should we get involved?"

He spoke so seldom, people got accustomed to excluding him from conversation. He sat silent, next to Isabella, moving in tandem with her, more like a Siamese twin than a shadow.

" Should we get involved? " It was a logical question.

" It 's the right thing to do," The others spoke in unison.

" I'm not so sure. In my case, the right thing to do is to keep Isabella out of anything which will not benefit her, and second, might harm her. Anybody who can squash a little kid and leave him to bleed to death in the street, is not someone I want her to get involved with. You do what you want, but leave us out of it."

He looked up at his mistress for approval. She gently scratched his neck. She knew his feelings, his loyalty. She also had a sense of right and wrong which kept poking its head up. She had not made up her mind .

Morty needed help. He knew exactly where to go.

Jerry burst through the door. He did not stop to

take off his coat, shake hands, nod to Isabella who he had not met before, but flung himself down on the floor, grabbed Moses and started a series of total body rubs which were ferocious.

" My legal partner! Don't forget. This little *putz* can put you all to shame." He got up. He took Isabella's hand and gave it a kiss. "You must be the Wicked Witch of the West who has captured my Morton Haberman's heart. Don't worry if you don't know who she is. You and I fly to *Alcapulco* tonight .All will be revealed on a surf-bound shore and magic moonlight. Morty, how did you find this beauty? You are too ugly to deserve her. She needs an Adonis like me. Now tell me, what brings me here on a gentle fall evening ?"

Mosie explained the details. Jerry kept silent, eyes closed.

" Is that all? First thing we do is get Gannon to sign a witnessed statement that he is the killer. Second, we work on the Pope to let Priests release criminals' confessions to the Police.Then, onto world peace and climate change. "

"I know what you are thinking, Jerry, but there is no reason to be sarcastic . There is a dead child whose killer is out there and who will go free if we do nothing ."

" Okay, folks, all kidding aside. There is only one way to get justice when your witnesses cannot speak. You bluff."

" Come with me. It is a fall afternoon . You are whizzing around a country road in your royal chariot. Your thoughts are below your belly button. You are not seeing everything you should be watching for. You hit a child. You see three witnesses who cannot testify.

" What if there is another witness? How can you be sure there isn't? It happened so fast. Another person who saw everything? One who is greedy for money. One who knows what a *Carrera* costs? He sends Chip a message. He demands money. He is your avatar. Let's call him Henry.

"Henry knows everything you folks know because he is all of you. Gannon knows Henry has to be real because only someone who was there, a witness, would know all the facts. He's a serious threat to Charlie . Gannon has two ways out. He either pays money forever, sums that exceed his ability to insure silence. A forever sword hanging over his head. Threats that could destroy his family, his life.

"Or, he decides to kill Henry. He can't be hanged twice. Just one more killing. What does it matter? We have him checkmated. He has to show up at the door with a briefcase full of cash, or a gun in hand, or both."

Jerry sinks to the floor and pulls Mosie down . " Well, partner, what do you think of the strategy?"

Morty looked at Jerry with mouth open. Never in his whole life, did he believe a brain could function with that speed or cunning. Jerry didn't even have to think before speaking. No wonder he got the big bucks. The solution came spilling out like an intermission between belly rubs on the floor. If you were blatantly guilty, you needed Jerry.

Isabella said nothing. She wondered if running her hands over his face would detect some anomaly to explain his ability.

Newton wasn't able to follow the logic as fast as his friends. When he did, he realized that he had better make sure Izzy had nothing to do with Henry. He did not like the ' kill Henry' even if he could keep his mistress out of it. His upbringing taught that if man wasn't able to punish the evildoers, then God would do it in due course. His job was not to serve Justice, but Isabella.

The dead silence warned Jerry this group was not comfortable with the plan . Time for the fall-back.

"Okay, folks, how about another suggestion from Uncle Jerry ? Our little furry friends locate every blond maiden whom Chips might have been with that afternoon? We send them all the same letter, that we were a witness to the accident. We suggest that they notify the Police of the incident, that they were an innocent passenger, Gannon was doing the driving, intoxicated."

"There could be dozens of girls. Gannon was quite a lêcher. Who does Henry send the letters to?"

" There is a book called ' Day of the Jackal."
A group of French ministers has a detective search for a murderer. One of them is leaking information to the criminal to help him elude the detective. The detective reveals the guilty minister by tapping his phone. When asked how he knew which minister to check, he says he tapped them all.

" We will do the same thing here. Henry threatens all of them. The ones who were home by the fire that afternoon will throw the letter out as a crank prank. The guilty one will pop up and go to the Police. Now, does Henry, we, write to Gannon or his concubines?

" Jerry, " Newton asked slowly and deliberately. "I see one flaw."

" Yes, my boy, there is one. I am surprised nobody else detected it."

" I was trained by the F.B.I. " the German Shepherd replied proudly.

" Tell us, oh all seeing master." Jerry teased.

" Well," back with his sonorous tones." If Henry writes to Gannon, we can set a trap; he's a goner. If the girlfriend gets the letter, scared and not knowing what to do, she tells Chips. He has get rid of her fast, so she doesn't getcold feet and report the accident. We could never know who was, only that her hidden murder saves Gannon. It makes more sense to attack Gannon directly."

It was a check and double check game. Heads going back and forth like a tennis match. The last serve settled the score. From a wet leafy country road, three blind dumb souls and their friends set in motion retribution.

*. *. *. *.

The ending was swift. As predicted, Gannon fell into the trap which closed firmly around him. The police had set up a meeting. Gannon arrived with both gun and money , prepared to resolve the threat to him by one way or another. There weren't many innocent explanations to offer the detectives videotaping him in the adjacent room.

Jerry Hermann was not in town when Gannon's family tried desperately to hire him. Somehow, he had foreseen the need of his services which he could not ethically refuse. Fortunately, he was not to be found, at least in the western hemisphere. A kibbutz, high in the Galilee, remembered him as one of their earliest student volunteers. They invited him back to see what advances they had made in the biogenetics of tomato plant desert horticulture, a subject always close to Jerry's heart.

The jury verdict was unanimous after one of the shortest deliberations on record. Chips, and his lovely looks and cute ass, would be lost to the female world forever.

The bitter episode slowly faded, except when the group would take a walk into the farmland north of the field. They missed little Donnie rushing out to greet them. It rekindled a memory they wished would go away .

Several months later, Mosie was scanning the Classified ads in the evening paper. " Listen to this," he read to his group. " There's a listing you might be interested in from *Automobiles for Sale*. 'The District Attorney has ordered for sale, on September 26 of this year, by Sealed Bid at Auction, of a 2021 white *Porsche* 911 *Carrera* convertible with black leather interior. Mileage 37,568. Needs body work. '"

Newton closed the conversation by intoning somberly. " What a great graduation gift. It's a guaranteed 'killer' car."

The Group did not find it funny.

CHAPTER THIRTEEN

'Morty faces family folly'

" Did you hear that?"

" No. Did you?"

" Must be a mouse."

" What else would be scurrying around here asking silly questions?"

" So, you must have heard it, too ?"

" Possibly. Maybe somebody's here."

" Did you hear anybody come in?"

" How can somebody be here if they didn't come in?"

" Who knows? Such are the mysteries of life."

" Wait. There it is again. No… it's not a squeak. It's not a bark. Not even a chirp. It's Morton Haberman!"

Morty hated to talk to the Quiros twins. Trying to get a word in edgewise, or even a letter at a time, was a futile exercise. They bantered the English language back and forth like a ping pong game, especially when they knew it was him. It was at least five minutes till they stopped for breath, got down on the floor on their backs , waved their arms and legs in the air, shouting ," Two. Four. Six Eight. Who don't we hate? Morty. Morty." They jumped up and gave him a communal hug.

They came from the same gene pool as Isabella, olive skin, jet black hair, round face and deep set eyes with long lashes. Damian was pudgy and Pythias skinny, which was a convenient way to tell them apart. What united them was an affection for Morty once they were convinced he was a stalwart companion for their vulnerable little sister.

" Well, little man," Pithy started to say.

" No! No! " Damie clutched his heart and swooned to the nearest chair. " Never say 'little' when thinking of our sister. She deserves 'big', even 'bigger'. "Biggest'. Yes, that's it. Morty, old man, are you a ' biggest'? We want Izzy to have a satisfactory sex life and ' biggest' is the best. Well? What's the answer? Give him a tape measure, Pithy. No… a yardstick! "

Morty had come over to ask a very serious question. He wondered if he would ever get the chance? They treated him as a volleyball, bouncing him back and forth, up and down, defying his attempts to reach ground and talk to them.

" Okay, Morton. How about some beer?"

"Damie, you shouldn't. You know what it says in the Bible, alcohol increases the desire, but takes away the ability."

" What about it, Morty? Is that true? Or did you come over to ask our permission to marry our sister ?"

If he married Isabella was there anyway he could ship her brothers off to Africa? He had to ask Jerry if a restraining order, lifetime ones ,could be issued by the Court. They were great guys . He could do worse. Their habit of treating Isabella like a little toy pet that belonged to them exclusively was something he would have to deal with.

" Okay, Morty, we give our consent. Now, was there anything important you came over to discuss?"

THUMP!!! Morty hit the ground…hard ! Morty was not a teetotaler. Beer sounded good.

" Okay. What do we have here? One rather ugly suitor for our treasure's treasure. I think he will do."

" The conditions. The Conditions. Don't be so hasty, brother dear." "

" Conditions? " Morty managed to get out.

" Did you hear an echo in the room? It's bad

enough trying to hear Morty dominate the conversation, but, to deal with his echo, too, is more than one can, or should, bear. Let's try again."

" The conditions..... conditions..... No, I don't hear anything. We're clear. Okay, Morty, Condition one."

" I don't understand this 'condition' stuff. Is it customary or are you just pulling my leg?"

" Pulling his leg? Did you hear that? Pulling his leg? Why would we want to take away one of the supreme pleasures of the conjugal bed? No. Pulling a leg is excellent foreplay. Cancel that. No, Morty, just listen.

" We have nurtured Isabella our entire lives. We have made her what she is. Did you expect to get her for nothing? "

" Well... I..."

" See, brother? He has no compunction to steal our sister's maidenhead, but when it comes to paying for it, he just hems and haws. I thought we warned Izzy always get a deposit in advance."

" 'Deposit'? Don't embarrass this lêcher. "

Despite their banter, Damie and Pithy looked serious and determined.

" Is this a family custom? Something the Catholic

Church requires? A municipal ordnance?"

" No. Morty. It's a joke. You know. Something to laugh at."

" I don't think any of this is funny."

" You will think it is funny when we get to Condition 2. Where are you going to live?"

" My house. It's old, but it's in good condition. Isabella likes it."

" We've been in it. It will do for a 'starter' house. You can't mean to live there permanently? It's got only one bedroom. Where are you going to sleep?"

Morty could not put a handle on the question. Why ask such a odd thing?

" In the bedroom, of course."

"Won't work."

" Why?"

" Four of us in bed together? Apt to get a little cramped."

" What ' four of us'? " Morty was starting to get angry.

" Pithy and me. Of course, you two. Just because you signed some little paper from City Hall, doesn't mean we'll give up protection of our sister ?"

" You damn well will !!! You will visit only on

invitation. I'm not having you butt-heads wandering around our house. It's off limits for you two."

" I think our little brother-in-law-elect is pissed. Okay, Morty. We give you that one , too. Now, Condition 3. How are you going to support Isabella ?"

This was a question Izzy and Morty had discussed on their own. This was serious stuff. Morty's income from the school was around $39,000 a year , before deductions. Isabella, working for a Catholic institution which rewarded with 50% cash/ 50% benedictions, took home for earthly sustenance,$ 43,000 before deductions.

" Okay, Morty. It'll do for a start."

Pleased to have finally gotten something they approved of, he objected, " What do you mean, 'for a start.'?"

" Babies." Pithy detected the bewildered look Morty. The poor guy was down for the count. " Let's leave the subject of how you two could have a baby around. We have pamphlets on the subject. Let's get to Condition 4. How are you going to raise the child ?"

This subject, too, had also been discussed by the two young lovers. He was going to tell them their thoughts on the subject, when he suddenly realized that there was a way out of their web . He opened the door and walked out

" My god," Pithy managed to get out. " The lover has balls, after all. We never even got to the other fourteen conditions. No sense wasting his beer." He divided the drink. " I just remembered. We can also cross out Condition Eleven. Morty is Jewish. He has to be circumcised. We better ask Izzy , just to be sure. She has a real delicate touch."

CHAPTER FOURTEEN

'Morty Loses his Job.........'

Joshua Cohen and Morty had a long history together. The trouble was, the man sitting in the chair in the Administration Office was not the Joshua Cohen of memory. The remembered Joshua Cohen was a short, severely over weight little Jewish boy with round face, early acne, bottle-thick glasses, unruly brown hair, stubby legs and arms, and a frightened posture. He was God's gift to the virile male high school students who required a daily punching bag to complete their academic curriculum. The number of times Morty needed to step in, pick him up from the ground, wash off his bruises, clean his clothes , offer a big hug and send him on his way, was countless

This Joshua Cohen was tall, maybe six feet two, lean with a muscular body outlined under a custom-cut silk wool suit. Contact lenses with a blue tint, eyes set wide apart, a sculptured facial contour with high cheek bones, thin lips and a clean almost beardless complexion completed the image. It was if the years of suffering had induced the Almighty to reward him with everything nature could offer. That, plus a career as the County's youngest District Attorney, the leading candidate for Mayor in the election to come, and a stunning wife whose family built most of the houses in the outer suburbs, completed the metamorphosis.

" Morty ," the god from Olympus invited him in and pushed a chair towards him. " Come in."

The voice was the same, albeit deeper and slower. Morty always had a hidden affection for Josh, feeling that the two of them were a kind of outliers, surviving on the kindness of strangers. They had not seen each other since the Reunion which Joshua used as a pre-election campaign test ground.

" Morty," Joshua started the conversation. " I insisted on this meeting. What I am going to tell you has to be private and not for public knowledge. I am going to ask you to promise to keep it secret."

" Whatever it is, I promise."

" I don't know if you keep up with politics in our city. The city is bankrupt. Since the old Moline Tractor plant moved out to China, half the town is on welfare. The other half refuses to pay taxes with all sorts of gimmicks. To survive, the city is planning to merge many of its departments with other cities in some sort of intra-county consolidation. Don't ask me what 's it all about or how it is going to work. I don't know. and I don't think anybody knows except for the whiz-kids from Washington who are masterminding this miracle."

He stopped. Morty wasn't sure how what this all had to do with him? Why did Joshua ask to see him?

" You are wondering what all this has to do with you? The County is going to consolidate the schools. The population is not growing. It is declining. Probably from the workers leaving for jobs elsewhere. Forward projections predict a drastic decline in students at every level. "

He paused and took Morty's hands in his. "Buchanan is on the chopping block. It is the oldest. It is the one which needs the most updating to satisfy new Codes and Regulations. Even when I was a student there , it needed repairs badly. The Boys' Room stank from leaky pipes. It 's going to close at the end of this semester, in a few weeks. "

" Where will the students go?

" They will be bused to whatever high school is closest to their home."

" Okay. The school is old, I give you that. It does

need fixing up. It should have had more things done instead of looking the other way. Things as they get old need care. That shouldn't be the reason to abandon them."

" Morty. You will be without a job, come June." One would have thought a tear or two glistened in the lawyer's eyes. " I will see what I can do to get you a job somewhere. Until I win the election, my hands are pretty much tied. If you will need any help for your family, come to me. I'll always be there for you." He stood up, gave Morty an affectionate hug and reluctantly left the the room.

When Morty left work for the day, it was slower than usual . He was saying a sad goodby to his home of many years.

*. *. *. *.

Supper that evening was not the usual chaos with everybody talking at once. Isabella had the unaccustomed chore of keeping conversation going. Morty had little to say once the bad news was released. Moses and Newton finished their meal quickly and retreated into the living room where they spoke in hushed worried tones to each other.

" It isn't the end of the world, Morty." Isabella said. " That's why I'm here. You have two of us now to take care of things. I'm sure this won't be the last time something serious hits us. Let's not panic. Let's see what what options we have."

" I don't have the education, the background, the skills you do, sweetie. It isn't fair to dump the burden onto you."

" Teaching some extra classes at night or applying to teach some remedial classes during the summer vacation , isn't really much of a burden. I often thought of doing that to earn some extra money even before we met."

" I could make some money doing yard work. I know most of the families. I will go over the Reunion list and give them a call." He gave Isabella a false smile and a strong hug."

"We'll manage. Don't worry. Finish your dinner. We'll put on some music and cuddle. I know some other things to take your mind off your problems. She gave his crotch an affectionate pat which Morty stopped objecting to. Life had certainly changed in the Haberman household.

The two pets had every reason to put their heads together. They lived there, too.

" I have some ideas, Newton. They may be a bit radical and difficult to carry out. They'ill need all the dogs. It 'll be a lot of work, but we owe it to Morty."

"Whatever it is, count me in. Isabella's happiness depends on Morty's."

"Let's schedule an Assembly on Saturday. We meet in the field instead of the park."

*. *. *. *. *.

Morty knew the pets were up to something important when Newton asked Isabella if he could attend the meeting. Happy to sit with Morty as he described a New Zealand *Blacks* rugby game, she was didn't mind. The game made no sense to her. It reminded her of the rough-and-tumble games she used to play with her older twin brothers, lots of bangs, falls, and bruises but it took Morty's mind off the bad news.

Moses explained to the Assembly the political decision to close Buchanan and how it affected Morty. They passed a unanimous decision to do whatever needed to help him. Moses outlined his Plan.

" Morty has not put away enough money to live on. He now has Isabella to think of. His only asset is the forty acres he preserved as a field for us. I want a thorough survey of the land, brooks, woods, ravines, hills. Also, any buildings which may be hidden from view by trees that have grown up. Any cellars from abandoned dwellings. Anything at all. Make sure to list where they are so Newton and I can investigate. This property has been around almost since the Revolution. Let's find something we can charge people to see. "

The dogs fanned out over the land. They climbed and dug. They unroofed three hundred years of artifacts, most of which were from the twentieth century. The pile of used condoms from hidden corners grew mightily, as did spent cartridge shells. The final inventory was delivered to the two leaders.

Moses scanned the list, nodding with each entry. Nothing aroused his interest until.... there it was.... what the little dachshund, Peter, had found by wriggling through a dense grove of azaleas annually ignored after dropping their flowers.

The sun had gone down. Moses and Newton thanked them all for their efforts. The two went inside for dinner. They needed sunlight in the morning to investigate what had been discovered.

CHAPTER FIFTEEN

'......... and Wins the World'

" This is what in the Middle Ages one would call a ' hillock.'

" Really?" Moses uttered a sarcastic exclamation wavering between exquisite joy and celestial disinterest .

" Yes, my dear companion. A 'hillock' is a small rise in the contour of the land, not quite a 'hill' and not quite a 'mound.'"

" The significance of such an erudite discovery?"

" Very simple, my dear Watson." Newton paused and sat down. " Think of its significance. It is 1669. The early settlers arrived. They viewed the virgin landscape. ' This is where I am going to plant my seed, but there are too many trees. The trees are good and I will use them to make a dwelling wherein I will disperse my seed, wife willing. '

"There is a problem. I will plow my land as I plow my wife. I need it smooth and level so not to tire my stalwart stallion. Let us pick some forty favored acres. Look, see there. I spy hillocks here, so I will skirt them with my plow and plant my seed in between, praying for a full harvest.

" God says to me, ' waste not, want not'. You have hillocks. I gave you hillocks. There is a reason. I could have made the land level, but I didn't. Now, use the damn things! So I do. I dig into them. I hollow them out. I find that they are clean, spacious and above all, blessed with an even cool temperature. Into some I put dairy products. In the winter, I carve big blocks of ice and place them deep in another hillock, cover the ice with piles of sawdust from the trees. I call that hillock my 'ice house'. I use it to make frappacinos in the hot summer which I sell to the Indians and my neighbors. In other hillocks, I place valuable tools and machinery to hide from the roving red-skinned pagans. Now, my ignorant friend we will open these caves of treasure and see what we find. Ahoy… Open sesame."

Newton was right. They found caverns with moldy sawdust, wrought iron tools, ceramic pitchers and crude dishware, pieces of furniture, and, best of all, a cornucopia of farm implements including a primitive one disc plow with harness for a horse or cow. With a careful study, the two were able to identify the items, except for one long board which puzzled Moses. It was about 5 feet long, 2 feet wide. Running along the top, were painted scenes from the Bible . " Look here," Newton demonstrated, " the colonists did not have paint with an oil base, so they used milk to hold the pigments."

Moses checked the length of the board. There was even Moses, with long beard holding the Ten Commandments. Everything was faded and peeling, yet visible.

" Milk?"

" Milk has casein which acts as a glue. Hasn't Morty ever used a bottle of *Elmer's Glue."*

" Okay. Why do you think there's a cow on the label? The glue was made from *Borden*'s cows.

" Newton, you are a fount of knowledge. How did you get so educated.? "

Newton blushed. " I just listened in to Isabella over the years. You still haven't guessed what the board was used for."

"Not a clue, big boy. Not a clue."

" Here's the kicker. When lusty colonial studs came courting in the winter, there was no central heating. The parents would put the young lovers in a bed with thick quilts over them. This historic relic was called a

' bundling board' and was inserted between them. Clever?"

Moses thought for a moment, running his eyes up and down the wood. " Fascinating. I wonder how many people today would pay to visit a real exhibit of life here centuries ago? Maybe rent some biblical wood?"

" Let's made sure we have catalogued everything hidden here and talk with Morty and Izzy."

*. *. *. *. *. *. *. *.

It didn't take any convincing to get Morty and Isabella on board. What amazed Moses was that Morty had a hidden entrepreneurial bone that never been aroused before. He jumped right in, throwing out suggestions and ideas like soaring fireworks. Was it the responsibility of his coming marriage, the shock of being fired, the enthusiasm of his companions, the passion to show that he would not be put down and tossed out, he became an unlikely rocket on it's way to the stars?

His first move was truly inspired. It happened one afternoon while the old colonial farm tools and equipment were lying out in the field, being washed. One of the abutter's children, who had been watching, asked Morty if he could touch the plow .Morty watched the child move the disc blade back and forth, cutting through the soil.

" Be careful. It might be sharp" Marty warned.

" It still works, ' the boy exclaimed. " It's not easy to do, but it cuts through."

Morty bent down and spread the trough. " That's just part of it. They had to put the seeds in what they called ' the furrow'. They rolled earth over it, watered it, dug out the weeds. It was a long hard process in those days. If you didn't do it, you starved to death."

"I have to get back home for supper. If I come back tomorrow, would you show me more?"

"If your mother says it is okay."

Morty was surprised when about ten minutes later, Slater returned with his mother.

" Thank you, Morty. It was lovely to have you spend this kind of time with Slater. It's unusual to see him so excited about something. Tomorrow afternoon is okay. I wonder.... would it be possible for you to have Slater over here for about four hours? I want to visit his grandmother over in Chillicothe . I can't get ahold of his regular babysitter.... that is ,if he won't be too much of a nuisance for you?" She saw Morty hesitate. " Of course, we wouldn't want you to go out of your way. We would pay you. Would twenty dollars an hour be okay? It's what we pay Colleen."

Morty started to protest.

" No. No. I insist. It's a bargain. All Colleen does is stick him in front of the t.v. Is it a deal? "

They shook hands. Morty went in the house and carefully marked the appointment on the calendar. He picked up his car keys. He drove into the center of the city. It wasn't until years later that Morty recalled that afternoon. Where two roads diverged in a wood, Morty had taken the path less trod, and that was going to make all the difference.

*. *. *. *.

The District Attorney's Office was such a busy, noisy, crowded, chaotic cauldron of people rushing, shouting, stopping and starting, carrying and wheeling files and boxes of lives and fortunes, Morty could not imagine how anything could be done to mete out Justice. He was about to leave having given up the possibility of cutting through the Gordian knot of chaos without a blowtorch, when Josh Cohen came out of one of the offices, yelling to the men following him, " No will do. Tell that fucking bastard it's my way or the highway....." He stopped , startled, " Morty! What are you doing here. " He turned to the secretary. " Let this man in whenever he comes. I don't care if I am screwing Jesus Christ's mother or even Jesus himself, but let him in." He saw the bewildered expression on the young girl's face. " Morty and I used to sneak down to Tijuana to get drunk. We used to fuck every hooker in sight as well as their ugly mothers. Oh, " He took Morty's hand and led him inside, calling back, " those were the old days. Be careful of him. He's dangerous, especially to virgins."

" Some water? Coffee? " He offered. "My secretary won't forget you. What brings you to this oasis of godliness? Isabella okay?"

" Josh," Morty stammered a bit," It's nothing serious. I just wanted to ask you about Buchanan."

" I wish I could change things and keep you on. "

" No. Nothing like that. The equipment. The tractors. The mowers. All that stuff. They'll all be left?"

" I was going to give you a 'heads up' on that, but this election is killing me. Do you want any of that junk? May be all of it? It's going to be dumped along with the wreckage from leveling the buildings."

" I do, Josh, that's what I was coming to see you about. I could pay something."

" Hell! Are you kidding? All that would do is louse up our antiquated city budget. Take it. Take it all," He started writing. " Here's a note. Take it to John Hermanson over in the City Assessor's Office, next floor up. It is my legal opinion that the equipment has no value and, as a good citizen, you have volunteered to remove it at no cost to the city . If he has any questions, come talk to me. So happy to see you and help you out. Let me know when you are growing some corn. I want to show my kids where food comes from. Take an election sign on your way out. Take two. Stick them around your house. " He picked up two ringing phones at the same time, mouthed 'good-bye' to Morty and held one receiver to each ear, while making horrible facial grimaces to each.

Morty felt a whole lot cleaner when he hit the exhaust-filled street.

CHAPTER SIXTEEN

' A happy ending for a happy book.'

Supper was more cheerful than a month earlier, especially after Morty revealed the increasing income from the Children's Recreation Center. They more than made up for his lost wages from the now derelict Buchanan High school. Isabella started a round of applause to which Newton exhorted a ' Hear! Hear! 'coda.

Morty picked up a spoon and clanked it on a glass. This, in itself, was an unusual occurrence. It immediately got everyone's attention.

"Ladies and gentlemen. As you have heard, things are going well. Profits are stable and increasing. The only suggestion I have is that we investigate the possibility of adding a geriatric facility. There are many families taking care of elderly parents. The children may have to duck out for a few hours to do errands, shop, personal needs. They worry about who will watch grandpa or grandma or both when they are gone? Who will give meds on time, keep the parents active, etc? We can offer such short term care. We install Bocci pads, shuffleboards, corn hole competitions, etc. If the weather is bad, we'll use a tent where we keep a small library, television, chess, checkers, card games , dominoes. We will have Port-a-Potties, coffee, cold drinks. We can add scenic walking paths. The dogs can accompany the clients and alert us if they fall or get into trouble.."

" Great idea, Morty. Let's add it."

" That is not why I called this meeting. So far, we have picked the 'low lying fruit '. Those are the services which are easy to do and have required a minimal financial investment. We can stay at this level. Or, " he paused for effect, " we can climb to a higher stage. One which promises greater returns, spreads a wider net, requires more employees, a deeper office backup, more overhead."

" What's the advantage, Morty" Mosie asked. " What do we have to gain?"

"Suppose, for the sake of argument," Morty looked across the table, " a national chain comes to town, and builds a facility with showers, hot tubs, a nutrition specialist, trained nurse or physician assistant, even a van with pickup and delivery? We may not have to close down. However, our profits could be seriously impacted to compete."

" How will your idea help?"

" When you hear what I propose, I think it will lift us higher in the feeding chain, give us a greater critical mass, and make it harder for anyone to hurt us. It is a gamble. Hear me out."

For the next hour, Morty spoke. He did not

rely on notes. He spoke smoothly, anticipating questions and objections. He developed a business plan which, if successful, would have moved their playground into the big times. All he needed was their vote. Their acceptance. As he said, it was a gamble.

*. *. *. *.

Damien was a dentist. Pythias an accountant .Predicting that Pythias would be less likely to get down on his all fours and welcome him with a wolf bark , Morty and Moses elected to do business in his office. They outlined the plan. It was unique to the area, but had been successful elsewhere.

" We need funds to buy old, out of commission, technologically obsolete , construction and highway machines. Machines which will have some life left in them, but not enough to make it profitable for companies to keep on their books. Trade-ins that are just dumped for new ones. We've scouted around. We know how many it will take for our needs and what it would cost to buy. The projected income." They showed the Proposal to Pythias. He nodded and pushed the paper back.

" How much money do you have?"

They showed him.

No comment. His facial muscles remained frozen like a mask. Finally, " I like your plan. It could work. You have to go into it fast, with all cannons blazing. If someone else gets wind of it, with more resources, you are fucked. Your greatest edge is that you thought of it first. Being first is a key advantage for success. Alexander Graham Bell applied for the telephone patent only minutes before his competitor showed up for the same patent. You need to get off your ass and scoop up all the derelict machinery you can find. It could work. Here's what we are going to do. "

" Thank you."

" Don't thank me until you hear my conditions. They are not negotiable. They are designed to protect Izzy. I will set up a corporation and put the playground in it. You and Isabella will be equal stock owners. Damie and I will lend the company the money you need for the expansion. You will give me your stock, half of the company, as collateral for the loan. You don't pay off the loan, you are out on your ass. You work for your wife and us the rest of your life. Understood? Be here tomorrow to sign. Same time. Agreed?" He did not hold out his hand."

Morty missed the 'woof, woof.' This was a different world. Mosie gave him a hug, They both needed it.

*. * *. *. *. *

Frank Hermanson must have kept his nose close to the prevailing election winds. They wafted favorably from the District Attorney's Office below him in the building. Even without a 'pass' from Joshua, he had no compunction offering the Buchanan soccer field bleachers, or whatever portion of them Morty wanted. They were removed to the forty acres before the sun had rotated once.

..*.*.*.*.*.

The upgrade was a brilliant success. The newly purchased machinery, cleaned , polished, some minimal rechroming, captivated the children.   Now there was something for the older customers. Once they had been vetted, and assigned a careful matched piece of equipment, they were let loose, to trench, to dig, to move, to topple piles, to build hillocks, to challenge invaders, to fight for territory, At night, with the spot lights flooding the field, through the dust and smoke, it appeared like a World War battle.   Morty even rented out old uniforms, helmets and gas masks to render a realistic touch. Smoke bombs were an expensive option. Morty discovered that some daddies liked to ride along with their children, but only if the kids approved . Adults paid extra.

Morty advertised on billboards, on the internet, in

the newspaper. He suggested to parents to give as a birthday present a few hours in the field. He got the approval of the *Veterans of Foreign Wars,* the *U.S. Army Recruiting Offices* and even the *French Foreign Legion*, all of which donated pennants and escutcheons to flutter on the light posts. Isabella had a local company sell teeshirts, caps, belts, sweatpants, backpacks with their logo.

Morty talked it up. What better way to burn off testosterone than a night at *Second Chance Fairgrounds?* After an hour-long documentary on a local television channel, Morty received an offer from a New York company which produced a traveling ice skating show inquiring about a franchise. Life was good, but needed to get better.

* *. *. *. *.

Between the telephone and Morty's pickup truck, the remainder of the shopping list was rapidly checked off:

Paint for the bleachers

Outdoor flood lights. These were left over after a California movie company had made a movie on the Chillicothe Massacre.

Microphone with strategically placed loudspeakers.

Pennants and flags all bearing the stars and stripes.

Card tables for the vendors selling ice cream, pastries, fried dough, pizza and coffee.

Portable neon signs to direct traffic and mark exhibits.

Trash pails with liners conveniently left over from the Buchanan High School.

Port-a-Potties . Try as he could, Morty could not discount these. He had to pay full rate.

The list went on and on.

The dogs were good at placing painted rocks to mark paths for direct traffic flow.

Morty had been leery of approaching Josh again, but the lawyer was enthusiastic to hold a re-election rally at the field. His *Committee to Elect Josh* even promised transportation for the elderly to and fro the field.

The local newspaper, its coffers bolstered by ads from Josh's campaign, was only too happy to send its junior reporters out , day after day, to document and print the preparations for the Grand Opening of the *Second Chance Family Fair.*

The only worry was the weather. Prayers to all permutations of God were offered daily in churches and synagogues whose members had fondly remembered Morty .

Finally, thanks to Isabella's effort, the *Saint Catherine Marching Band and Chorus* agreed to open the proceeding with selections from Sousa and Queen.

Everything was set in motion. There was to be only one more surprise. Who else but Moses would be selected to perform it?

CHAPTER SEVENTEEN

Fear and trepidations ruled the family home. What if it rains? What if nobody shows up? What if people laugh at us?

" What if bubonic plague sweeps the county? That is my real fear, " intoned Newton, fed up with the doom-sayers

Everyone laughed, which broke the tension.

" You know," Isabella offered, " If nobody shows up Morty and I will stay home and have some unprotected sex for starters. You miscreants can find your own corners to misbehave."

" Izzy, I don't think that needs to be a topic of table conversation, "Morty objected.

" Are you really considering that?" Moses asked, worried.

" If we are, how does that affect you, my friend?"

" YOU ARE? You better get married first. I will never be able to hold my head up Saturday morning at Assembly. I think separate bedrooms are the rule from now on. "

"It's time to leave, folks," Newton pulled on his

harness. Our audience awaits."

If the audience had been waiting, they were having a rousing time. The Band welcomed them at the gate, playing all the songs from the past, as well as some which made no sense to the eldercare contingent but elated the nubile newbies.

Jerry Hermann had volunteered to be the Master of Ceremonies. His booming voice ricocheted across the field, hitting and banging the same words coming back from the scattered speakers .

" Don't forget the Ice House . You'll never see one of those again in your life time. Frozen ice cream for sale in the tent. Check out the hillocks. I have it on confidential reports that Captain Kidd sailed up the Ohio river to hide his loot from Spanish galleons in one of them. The first guest to find a gold doubloon gets to keep it. Ladies. Can you fit into a wonderful dress found in Hillock no. 6? It is a size 2, according to our local historian Mrs, Ledecky. Take off your clothes and try it on. Nobody will watch except teenage monsters. If it fits, let us know. Mrs Talmadge of Anseth Street has a booth in the tent ready to make your own custom size.

Imagine surprising your boyfriend or husband ?

Remember, no one wore bras in those days. Hurry. Hurry. Ten minutes left. Ten minutes to go. Hurry to the bleachers. The *Grand Processionale* will be starting. Don't miss it. The *Grand Processionale.* See your sons and daughters as they want to be seen, all grown up. Beer in the tent. Be amazed. This is what it all comes down to. Get to the Bleachers. I hear the band. Line up in back of them. They will lead you in. "

Jerry was a natural. No wonder he could get Blackbeard off with a misdemeanor, and Jesus with 30 days of community service picking up beer cans near Nazareth.

Suddenly the band broke out with *Hail to the Chief.* A crowd of singing adults swung in behind the band . Leading them, pulled on a dog cart by four stately Dalmatians was Joshua Cohn waving kisses.

The parade entered the cleared field between two rows of bleachers. The band took their places in the front row. Marching four abreast, the pets of the city, freshly groomed , wagged their tails as they passed by. The abutters came next, holding a banner advertising their victory over Warfield. Mrs. Belasco danced in with poms poms and a sequined skin-tight body suit , holding a sign, *Abutters for Puppies.*

Everybody stood up and applauded when their children came in. They were not walking. They were not running. Everyone of them was seated on a piece of machinery, all painted and polished to gleam in the spotlights. On command, their sons and daughters all stood up , gave their parents a big dignified bow and salute and rode off, in complete and skillful command of their humungous chariots .

The lights dimmed. The band rose to their feet. *The Wedding March* filled the air as Morty and Isabella slowly walked in, accompanied by Newton. Without anybody being aware of it, some of the parents had placed a low platform on the field, between the bleachers.

Waiting for them on the platform was a Buddhist monk, the end result of hours of negotiations. He wore a Jewish shawl cloth and a high Roman Catholic collar. Despite this cornucopia of religious symbols, the myriad details to merge one Jewish male with one Protestant maiden had been transformed into a Certified Marriage Certificate down at City Hall by Jerry Hermann .

The ceremony was historic and clear. The two lovers spoke to each other. Rings were exchanged.

Then everything stopped. People looked around to see what was going on.

Trotting into view with a white package in his mouth was Moses. Slowly, deliberately, with no embarrassment or hesitation, he stepped up into the platform. He laid the white napkin neatly at Morty's foot. The new husband smashed his foot down on the glass cup, shattering it .

The audience could not be certain if the sound memorialized the rupture of Izzy's maidenhead two months ago or the destruction of the Jerusalem temple two thousand years ago, but to Morty and Izzy and Mosie and Newton, time was just beginning for their lives together.

THE END

coming soon :

The further adventures of Morty and Moses.

www.ingramcontent.com/pod-product-compliance
Lightning Source LLC
LaVergne TN
LVHW010057170826
845678LV00012B/2154